—SKY KING—
AND THE
GREAT SOLAR STANCE
MY TRANSFORMATION INTO THE SEVEN HEADED ANGEL

Sky King

And

The Great Solar stance

Copyright © 2025 by Vernon Gilmette

All rights reserved. No part of this book may be reproduced, stored in a retrieval system, or transmitted in any form or by any means—electronic, mechanical, photocopying, recording, or otherwise—without prior written permission of the author, except for brief quotations used in reviews or scholarly works.

This book is a work of nonfiction. While it reflects the author's own experiences and recollections, some names and identifying details have been changed to protect the privacy of individuals.

For inquiries or permissions, contact:

Vernon Gilmette

Skygod1975@gmail.com

ISBN: 979-8-218-83204-9

Printed in the United States of America

First Edition

Zevyn Publishing

Cover Design & Photography by Ronnie Johnson

Dedicated to my loving mother, Carol Andrade

And to the everlasting memory of my father,

Donald Gilmette Sr.

May the Universe be pleased with you Dad.

Contents

The Genesis 1

The B-Boy Stance 7

Education 11

The Golden Era Begins 16

1988 23

Duane Darock 32

The Show 36

Beat Box Paul 40

DJ Super V 43

The Four Track 46

Law School 50

Basics Of Organized Knowledge 54

Tim Fim 56

Five Towns College 60

These Tu Bum Emcees 77

The Ensoniq EPS 81

Scotty Watt 85

The Raid 87

Revolutionary Minds 91

Digital 95

Seven Headed Angel 97

The E.P 102

The S.H.A Album 113

The 3rd Eye Open 119

Amherst 121

Two Giants and the Birth of Sky King 123

Solo Albums 136

The Korg Triton 141

The Day The Earth Stood Still 145

I Came to Destroy Your Civilization 152

Rkeyology 160

Civil War 162

Seven Headed ARSTO 167

Golden Soul 172

Evil Jesus 185

The Reunion 198

The Holocron 206

The Epilogue 215

Foreword

By

Demmene Syronn

Schenectady, New York, was where I first met hip-hop. Not in the sense that the culture was born there, but in the sense that my exposure to it helped create me. By the mid-1980s, I was still too young to be running the block. My older cousins carried that role, and I lived vicariously through them. From the vantage point of my grandmother's porch, I absorbed it all. From those steps, I witnessed a cultural shift unfolding in real time. Schenectady in the 80s was alive—girls turning ropes in Double Dutch, dice games rattling on corners, dudes constantly tuning up pedal bikes, and the inevitable street fights that broke out from time to time. At the center of it all was the music. It wasn't just background noise; it was the pulse, the soundtrack to an entire scene.

The summer of 1986 is burned into the fabric of who I am. Tracks like Check Out My Melody and Eric B. Is President weren't just songs—they were anthems you couldn't escape.

Imagine being twelve years old, catching the low rumble of bass drifting from the top of the block, the sound swelling with every second until the source came into view: someone strolling slow, like they owned time, balancing a twelve-pound boombox with three seven-inch speakers, pumping out the freshest sound you had ever heard.

Burgundy Adidas tracksuit catching the sun, shell toes to match, each step deliberate, almost regal. The air vibrated with synergy. It was as if this new energy carried a strange familiarity, something that felt both groundbreaking and rooted at the same time. These young men, gliding down the sidewalk with effortless cool, were my superheroes. They didn't need capes or comic book powers—their gift was carrying the soundtrack of a movement. That was my initiation into culture: not from textbooks, not from documentaries, but right there on the block, through vibrations in the air and the styles of the people who lived them.

Even then, I began to sense the difference between people who dabble in hip-hop and people who are hip-hop. It's a visceral knowing; the same way a college scout can watch a ball player dribble once and instantly tell he's got the gift. Some folks can mimic the clothes, learn a few moves, even spit a rhyme or two. But when someone speaks the core language of the culture, it's undeniable. You hear it. You feel it. You just know.

That sensibility—the "scout's eye"—stayed with me. It shaped how I listened, how I created, and what sparked my interests. After college at UMass Amherst, where I linked with Tem Blessed and DJ Walt G to form Busted Fro, I made the decision to move to New Bedford, Massachusetts, to take music more seriously. That city had its own rhythm, steeped in Cape Verdean and Portuguese culture. The accent, the flavor, the cadence of the people—all of that found expression in their artforms. It wasn't what I had grown up with in Schenectady, but it was authentic in its own way.

Around that same time, Busted Fro was invited to contribute to a compilation album called Revolutionary Minds. For us, it was monumental—our first professionally recorded songs, "Tem Blessed Blast" and "Fire and Ice," both produced by me. As proud as I was of our work, there was one track on that record that truly captivated me: The Combat Show by Ricky Culture, produced by someone credited as God V. That track radiated authenticity. The whole vibe was razor sharp, but the beat in particular was undeniable. It was the kind of production that instantly made me wish I had been behind it. Later, I would learn that God V was none other than Sky King. That was the spark. My ear told me: this was somebody who gets it.

Not long after, I caught an episode of a local TV program called Put Out The Word. The episode featured the group Seven Headed Angel. Watching them, everything clicked. Seven Headed Angel wasn't just a crew—they were a force. Raw, magnetic, unapologetically authentic. They embodied hip-hop in a way I recognized instantly. And at the center of it all was the Supreme B-boy himself, Sky King.

From that moment forward, my respect for him only deepened. What struck me then, and still strikes me today, is that Sky King glows with blinding authenticity. He doesn't imitate hip-hop; he is hip-hop. He carries the same fluency, the same rootedness that I first felt as a kid on my grandmother's porch. That essence can't be faked—and he's had it all along.

This book is the story of how he became who he is—artist, leader, producer, culturalist, healer, and true B-boy. It's a record of a life lived inside the culture, not around it. And for me, both as a fan and a friend, it's been an honor to witness.

I'm thankful that people like Sky King still walk among us. Because individuals like him are cultural treasures—living embodiments of a time and energy that grew into one of the greatest artistic, cultural, and business movements of the last hundred years. Hip-hop changed the world, and people like Sky King remind us why.

This is his story. This is the world of Sky King.

Chapter One
The Genesis

Dec. 20th, 1975. Westlawn Housing Projects, New Bedford, MA.

When I was born, my family lived at 193 Liberty St., in the red building beside the rent office. My brother Kippy and I shared a room, my sister Audra was across the hall, and my parents' bedroom was downstairs.

Sometime in 1979, I was at the park with the red slide. Westlawn is split in half by Maxfield Street, the northern half has the red slide park, and the southern half has the green slide park. I was playing when I saw a kid banging on the side of a porch with a stick. I walked up to him and asked if he wanted to be my friend. He said yes. That's how I met my first rhyme partner, my brother for life, Nathan Monteiro.

Sky King

In the spring of 1980, I found out we were moving out of Westlawn. I was devastated, thinking about not seeing my friends anymore and having to meet new ones. I cried—the whole shebang. Then my mother told me my father had bought a house across the street. What? Across the street? That meant I could still hang out and play in Westlawn. I was good after that. We moved to Sycamore St., six houses up from Liberty. My brother and I weren't sharing a room anymore—that must have been lame for him, considering he was 11 years older than me. But I was chilling. Everything was cool.

About two years later, Grandmaster Flash & The Furious Five dropped *The Message*. I was only six years old in 1982, almost seven, my birthday is in December. Even at that young age, I was completely blown away by Melle Mel. Something about the way he rhymed felt serious, nothing silly or gimmicky. He painted pictures, but not with paint. He painted that shit with words. Crazy. But weirdly, listening to Mel didn't immediately lead me to emceeing. Maybe I was too busy trying to breakdance or some other shit. *Planet Rock* by Soul Sonic Force was dominating the cardboard wars in Westlawn. Mark Bark was famous for recreating that classic beat on his chest. He would hit that thing hard. The Message was my favorite joint at that time. But in about a year, all that will change.

Seven years old. I was walking to Westlawn, heading to Nate's crib. I only lived six houses away, a twenty second walk. As I crossed Liberty St. and hit the sidewalk, I heard this crazy drum breakdown. The volume was bananas. The breakdown was followed by a hard-hitting drum pattern. Mark Canary, who lived in the red unit on Maxfield, was blasting that shit. I heard it clear as day from the Flagpole (the flagpole is old school Westlawn). The flag was right where Sycamore and Liberty intersect. Then I heard the first bars of the song that would alter the course of my life:

"Two years ago, a friend of mine, asked me to say some MC rhymes. So, I said this rhyme I'm about to say, the rhyme was def, and then it went this way…"

It was the first time I heard *Sucker MCs* by RunD.M.C. I needed to know who and what this was. I walked toward the music, peeped Mark in the window, and asked him who it was. He told me "Run-D.M.C.," but I was young, and the music was blasting. I thought he said "Ron Di Emsy," like it was someone's first and last name.

I ran straight to Nate's. I told him I heard a new song by a dude named Ron Di Emsy. He told me he had been listening too. One of us—I can't remember who—ended up with it on tape. We finally figured out it was RunD.M.C., and that it was two rappers. There were two of us. Nate was Run. I was D.M.C. We recited the lyrics but changed words, acting like we wrote them. Then the big idea popped up: Why don't we write our own raps?

I was around eight. Nate was nine. He said his rhyme name was Jam O Ski. I said mine was Mic O Dee. I got the D from D.M.C. because I always said his verse. We had a few silly, half-ass routines we would do, but nothing written. We were basically rehashing Run-D.M.C. and Kurtis Blow verses. It was time to step it up. We wrote our first rhyme:

> I'm Mic O Dee and I'm Jam O Ski...
> We rock the house in the place to be...
> It's '83 and we're kicking it live...
> Then it's '84, then it's '85...
> I'm Mic O Dee and I'm here to say...
> Rhymes like these we do every day...
> We take the bus, the crowd jumps on us...
> We devastate the nation with our own creation...
> Now my name is Nate but call me Jam O Ski...
> I rock the house most definitely...

I can't remember the rest. That was my rebirth. I was born again. My first step into the world of verbal arts. But rap wasn't my only love. If rhyming was my girlfriend, I was cheating on her with Kung Fu Theater. Whatever I was doing on Saturdays from 12 to 2 p.m. got instantly put on hold. Nothing was more important than kung fu flicks. Shiiiiit... Nate and I thought we were official Grandmasters. We were flipping all over the crib. Chucks, Chinese stars—all that fly shit you could get downtown at Oriental Imports. My pops even bought me a ninja suit. The whole nine—the tabby boots, everything. It even came with ninja claws. Real metal, sharp as hell. We tried climbing trees with them, but we weren't strong enough. Those things were dangerous.

Then the Universe corrected course. It felt like it didn't want me to veer off the path. Something marvelous happened. My brother got two turntables, a mixer, a receiver amplifier, a tape deck, an equalizer, and speakers. This was the greatest thing that could've happened to me at that time.

My brother Kippy—my only maternal brother—was a monster. A superstar athlete. Boxing, football, track. And he had serious hands. Knock dudes out. Nobody played with Kip. He was in shape too—straight bodybuilder status. When Kip first got his set, the very first thing he said to me was, "DO NOT TOUCH MY SHIT. IF I CATCH YOU TOUCHING MY STUFF, I'M GONNA KICK YOUR ASS." He meant that.

But when he left the house every day, what do you think I did first? Yep. Touched his shit. I figured out how to turn everything on and got busy. Kip had mad records, but I didn't really play those. I rocked my parents' albums—James Brown, Isaac Hayes, Billy Paul, and Bobby Blue Bland. I have a vivid memory of rocking Papa's Got a Brand-New Bag, flashing that famous horn Kool Moe Dee would later sample for *How Ya Like Me Now*.

I had to remember exactly how Kip had all his dials and faders. One mistake, and it would be curtains for me. He caught me a few times. He busted my ass. One time, I ran into the bathroom but couldn't close the door fast enough. We had one of those old clawfoot bathtubs. I tried to wedge myself between the tub and the wall, but that shit didn't work. He was hooking off on me—all body shots. Tore my ass up.

Mind you, Kippy was eleven years older than me. He was nineteen, flaming off on me. Crazy. But even beatdowns couldn't stop me. I loved music too much to be deterred by an ass-whipping. I just had to get better at sneaking into his room—and not getting caught.

Chapter Two
The B-Boy Stance

June of 1984 is when my hip-hop education really took off. Kippy and my youngest paternal brother, Boo (who was still eight years older than me), took me to see Beat Street. While the opening credits were still rolling, I had to use the bathroom. Boo took me, and before we got back to our seats, he stopped me. He told me to fold my arms across my chest and place my feet at a certain angle. Then he said, "This is the B-Boy stance. This is how the fresh kids stand." He had no idea that would be embedded into my psyche for the rest of my life.

That pose became the cornerstone of my being. It conveyed supreme confidence in whatever I had going on or a total lack of confidence in whatever you were trying to display. Whenever a kid was on the cardboard getting busy, I was suede Puma-ed down in the B-Boy stance because Boo told me to. No bullshit.

Beat Street was crazy to me. In a weird way, I felt like Lee, the young star of the film. My brother Kip was a DJ like

Sky King

Double K, and his best friend Ricky was a Puerto Rican graffiti writer like Ramo. I can't even make this stuff up. Shit was ill. The fly part was when Double K DJ'd the jump-off in the condemned building, and they had to hook up the electricity to the pole outside. Lee comes in and does his little popping routine to *Looking for the Perfect Beat* by The Soul Sonic Force. Then Kuriaki comes in and flames off with the crazy floor rock to *Planet Rock*.

Powerful Pexter says, "You're a biter. All your homeboys are biters. You're wack. So, what's up with that?" That scene was hip-hop in its purest form.

There was some lame shit in Beat Street, but the overall package had me mesmerized. I hated the battle in the subway, but the battle at the Roxy??! When Lee says, "Bronx Rockers... Chino... come on!" Yooo. What's more B-Boy than the way the Bronx Rockers and Beat Street swarm the floor? Hip-hop is such a beautiful culture.

Then it happened. Melle Mel rocked the Beat Street Breakdown at the end of the flick. Double K just did a Milli Vanilli to Mel's first verse. But that second verse? That was like Superfly Snuka jumping off the top rope. For months, I kept asking Kippy if he had that record yet. I was pissing him off. I saw Beat Street like twenty times— no bullshit. I had Melle Mel's lyrics memorized before I even had the joint on wax or cassette. Those rhymes were way beyond what Run-D.M.C. was doing. Mel was my champion. Too intelligent. Too sophisticated.

The Great Solar Stance

1984 was a huge influence on me. And so was my mother. She was always playing music. She had her own stereo in the living room and was constantly putting me onto new sounds. The summer of '84 was monumental. Sundays were cleaning days, and one Sunday, I heard something I hadn't heard before. *Smooth Operator* by Sade was on blast. I ran downstairs to find out what it was. The album was *Diamond Life*. When I looked at the cover, I immediately fell in love.

Plus, I was fixated on this different melodic soundscape—soft, inviting vocals gently riding over the instruments. That's when I first started paying attention to snares. I didn't know it at the time, but Sade would become one of the foundations of my production style. Instead of playing that album on my mom's stereo, I would sneak into Kippy's room and play it on his setup because he had a better-quality sound. I risked getting fucked up just to listen to Sade. I would stare at that album cover for what seemed like an eternity. I'm surprised I never learned to play an instrument. Listening to that album felt like the band was right in front of me. Sade is most definitely part of the Sky King starter kit.

At some point in '84, Boo and I were at my grandma's house on Cape Cod. It was late—like midnight or something. We were watching TV, and New York Hot Trax came on. I had heard about the show, but I had never seen it. The host introduced a new group called The Fat Boys. They did a live performance of a song called *Human Beat Box*. That shit completely blew my wig off. Buff's beatbox was nuts. Markie

Sky King

Dee and Kool Rock Ski got their shit off. I swore up and down that these dudes were the truth. Run-D.M.C. better watch out because these cats were breathing down their necks. I couldn't wait to get back to New B so I could tell Nate about The Fat Boys.

Next thing you know, I'm walking around doing my little bullshit beatbox. I sucked at that shit. Had to leave it alone. If I thought Kip was pissed because I kept asking for that Beat Street soundtrack, then Boo must've been hot because I was on his heels checking if he got that Fat Boys tape yet. Since my youth, I've always been eager to get the newest music.

Whodini dropped their album *Escape*. The rapper Jalil was dope. I really didn't care for Ecstasy, even though I found out years later that Jalil wrote all his rhymes. In '84, I was eight turning nine and paying serious attention to these lyrics. Kurtis Blow put out *Ego Trip*, and I thought that shit sounded crazy artificial. I was never a big Kurtis fan. *AJ Scratch* was cool, but the rest of that joint was corny. Even at that young age, I could see that with my eyes closed. The Treacherous Three killed the Christmas show in Beat Street, so I gave their album a chance. I wasn't impressed.

I'm a tough crowd. It takes a lot to impress me. Even now in my forties, I'm still the same. I'm glad I had all this music readily available. I didn't know any other kid my age who had an in-house DJ. '83 and '84 was when I began to accumulate the ingredients I needed to cook up the Sky King stew.

Chapter Three
Education

In 1985, LL Cool J released his debut album, *Radio*. Run-D.M.C. dropped *King of Rock*. That album was wack. The title song was dope, but everything else was weak. These dudes were my heroes—how could this happen?

But that LL shit? That was hitting. He was like a fusion of Melle Mel and Run-D.M.C. LL was no joke on the mic—powerful poetry, an insane amount of energy. This dude was a fireball. His arrogance was through the roof, and I think that it rubbed off on me. Later, when I really started emceeing, I couldn't wait to tell the world how everybody else sucked. That was a bad trait I had. Saadiq wasn't fond of it. I'll get into that later.

The Radio album had some HARD joints on it. That shit would get you amped up. Straight battle rhymes. He was not playing at all. LL was younger than Run-D.M.C., and he had that youth on his side, ushering in a more complex way of rhyming. It was still that old-school style—rocking over a drum beat with a DJ scratching a hit noise—but his lyrics were more intricate.

A mere two years after Run-D.M.C. had changed my life, I was already starting to phase them out as my go-to rhyme guys. But Run and D still had that back-and-forth style—they had mastered that shit. Later, I found out that Lil Rodney C and Kevy Kev Rockwell (Double Trouble) had accused them of biting their style.

Then Krush Groove hit theaters in '85. Run-D.M.C. was on top of the world. LL and The Fat Boys were in the flick. It was dope at the time. But lyrically, Run-D.M.C.'s reign wouldn't last much longer. Within the next few years, they would be entirely shut out of the game. I'm speaking strictly about emceeing—not record sales. Shit... 1986 brought them their biggest hits.

But back in '85, you had a young LL coming for their heads. You had The Fat Boys gunning for them. And then, out of nowhere, we got this storyteller—*La Di Da Di* dropped, and Slick Rick busted on the scene. A completely new and unique style. I was studying and soaking all this in. I didn't just listen to the music—I studied the lyrics and broke everything down.

Doug E. Fresh was in Beat Street, so I was already hip, but I wasn't really a fan of his beatboxing. I thought Buffy was much better. MC Ricky D was unorthodox—his accent, his word choices, everything made him stand out. I've always had a strong attention to detail—the little things, the small inflections here and there—that's what I was focused on. I understood what made one emcee different from another.

Nate and I weren't writing all the time—just now and then, when we were bored. But when I was home alone with Kippy's records, that's when I would do my analysis. I was gathering all the right seasonings. The Sky King soup was slowly coming together. There were many iterations of myself before I became Sky King. This was the early stage.

Music production wasn't even on my radar. I liked playing around with little Casio keyboards, but that was it. I noticed that Doug E. and Rick went with more orchestrated instrumentation—like Whodini and The Fat Boys—rather than the TR-808 drum machine sound that was the foundation of Run-D.M.C. and LL's production. Years later, I found out that Teddy Riley produced The Show. It was probably listed on the vinyl, but I didn't know who Teddy was back then. I didn't start reading the credits until about '87.

That classic SHIH SH SH SH SHIH shaker on that joint was dope. Teddy could've used an 808 for all I knew, but it wasn't those hard rock-band drums. I noticed tiny things like that, but making beats wasn't even a thought for me yet.

Then Schoolly D dropped *P.S.K. What Does It Mean?* and *Looking at My Gucci* in '85. Those beats were bananas. The drums on P.S.K. were the flyest shit out to me. I didn't think Schoolly was the dopest emcee, but his delivery rode those tracks perfectly. He was innovating— I must give him that. That was the first gangsta rap I know of. Ice –T took Schooly's whole style and made his *6 In the Morning* joint. Just-Ice's *Latoya* didn't drop until '86, and he wasn't rocking any gangsta rhymes on that joint.

All this music meant something to me. In the very core of my being, I felt like I needed to be a part of this movement. I needed to participate in this movement. It wasn't just the music—it was the culture. The way I carried myself, the way I spoke, the way I walked—it was all influenced by this culture. In 1985, I was nine turning ten, and these were the thoughts bouncing around in my head. Kippy was an athlete. My best friend Nate was an athlete. Most of the kids in Westlawn Projects were athletes. We played Fumble every day. Paul Gonzalez (Ricky the graffiti writer's younger brother) was usually our steady quarterback. I could play football, but I didn't stand out like Nate did. We played basketball all the time. I sucked at ball. All I cared about was music and kung fu flicks.

Across the street from Westlawn was The Boys Club. That's where you'd find all the young athletes and all the other young B-Boys from New B. It was mostly kids from the West End, but there were dudes from the North and the South too. That's where you found out who was nasty at breaking, who could rap, and who could beatbox.

The Boy's Club was the shit. Everybody went to the Club. Too many memories. Those were the fucking best times. WORD!!

The Great Solar Stance

I remember when UTFO dropped *Roxanne, Roxanne*. I was at the Boy's Club the first time I heard it. It didn't take Kip long to get the album—he had all the joints. I think *Roxanne, Roxanne* hit in '84, but UTFO's album dropped in '85. That joint set off the Roxanne Wars. Roxanne Shanté came with Roxanne's Revenge, and a bunch of tracks followed. That might be the first rhyme battle on wax that I was aware of.

The concept of battling was dope. Shanté had a fly, aggressive style—an official emcee. Way better than a lot of the dudes out.

Things were changing fast. You had to have your own style—something different. If you couldn't adapt, you couldn't compete. That was clear to me. At nine or ten years old, that was clear to me.

Nate and I stopped using those dated names. No more Mic O Dee and Jam O Ski. Since Nate used to call me VG (because of my initials), I just went by Vee Gee, and Nate became MCN, or MC Nate. We kept it simple. When it comes to certain things, sometimes less is more.

Chapter Four
The Golden Era Begins

1986 was about to be a pivotal year for rap music. I won't go into all the details of that time, but I'll speak on the key moments that shaped my rap future.

Run-D.M.C.'s *Raising Hell*, the Beastie Boys' *Licensed to Ill*, Just-Ice's *Back to the Old School*, and Doug E. Fresh's *Oh My God* were the albums that steered my daily rotation. Tracks like *Peter Piper*, *Paul Revere*, and *Latoya* were my anthems. I always felt Latoya was a *La Di Da Di* bite, but I rocked with it anyway. It was dope.

Then I heard Marley Marl and MC Shan's *The Bridge*. From that moment, I knew everything before '86 would be considered old school. That year, sampling revolutionized rap, and no one did it better than Marley Marl. The grittiness of the production on The Bridge altered rap music as I knew it.

BDP responded with *South Bronx*, and KRS-One's style hit different—it felt pure. Shan answered with *Kill That Noise*, but BDP shut it all down with *The Bridge Is Over*. The illest diss track my ten-year-old ears had ever heard. Shan couldn't

The Great Solar Stance

respond. The beat, the rhyme, the hook—everything about that joint was inspiring. Raw, stripped down to the essence. Pure Hip-Hop.

But nothing inspired me more than the day my brother Boo walked into the house and told me to listen to these new joints by Eric B. The look on his face as he pulled that cassette out of his pocket told me everything I needed to know. It was going to be crazy. When I heard *Eric B. Is President* and *My Melody*, my life changed forever. NO BULLSHIT. No emcee had hit my central nervous system like Rakim did. I must've played those two songs a million times that day. Boo's tape became my tape.

Rakim was a scientist. Like Spoonie Gee, Kool Moe Dee, and my guy Melle Mel all rolled into one. Nate instantly became a Rakim fan too. We knew we had to step our game up. Our rhyme-writing went into overdrive. No fake shit—analyzing rap was what I liked to do. It was what I loved to do. While playing with G.I. Joe and Star Wars figures, I was also dissecting rap lyrics with a fine tooth comb. Anyone who really knows me knows this is the truth.

Nate and I weren't just writing rhymes; we were trying to write songs. We had no beats, just words. This was the era of ending your verse with the song title. We had a joint called *We Can Do This*. I don't remember the rap, but I remember coming up with the title while writing at my kitchen table. Moments like that stick with me forever.

Sky King

I wanted to record a song. We finally convinced Kip to let us make a tape. I begged him constantly, and he kept shutting me down. I guess I wore him out. He got tired of me sweating him. Kip told me to get a blank tape. But all my tapes were filled with music. I don't have any blank tapes. The only option was my Eddie Murphy Delirious tape. That was my shit. Nate and I cracked up to it regularly. But we had to record this joint, so I stuffed toilet paper into the holes on top of the tape. That's that old-school shit young cats don't know about.

I handed the tape to Kip, and he threw on the instrumental to *Play It at Your Own Risk* by Planet Patrol—basically *Planet Rock* with more piano. Kip didn't have a mic, so we did the only thing we could: plugged headphones into the mic jack. That was some Return of the Boom Bap album cover type shit. Kip hit record, let the beat rock, and we went in full blast. Straight-up full-back-hitting-the-hole status.

He stopped us. "Hold on, fellas. Slow down, relax. You guys aren't even on beat." He had to coach us. We were crazy eager. I just wanted to hear my voice on tape. After some instruction, we finished the joint in one take, passing the headphones back and forth. You could hear our voices fading in and out as we handed each other the ghetto mic. Kip must've been happy to get us the fuck out of his room.

I played that song repeatedly. Hearing my voice for the first time was weird. It didn't sound like what I thought in my head. The track had no hook, just beats and rhymes. Nobody knew Nate and I rapped. I was kind of shy with it. We kept it

The Great Solar Stance

low-key. I'd get my backspin off at The Boys Club, but I wasn't letting anyone know I was rhyming.

One day in sixth grade, I was talking to my man Charles Perch (nickname: Toona). Delirious came up, and I told him I had it on cassette. He asked me to borrow it, so I let him. I completely forgot my joint was on it. The next day, he came in like, "Yo... what the fuck was that at the beginning?" Ah shit—the cat was out of the bag. I told him it was me and Nate from Westlawn. "Nate Monteiro?" he asked. Turns out, they went to Carter Brooks Elementary together in second grade. Small city type shit. Toona teased me forever about that joint. I thought he'd show everybody, but he didn't. That's my man.

My sixth-grade situation was tricky. I let Hip-Hop dictate my education path. In fifth grade ('85-'86), I took an Accelerated Education Assessment Test. My high scores led Carney Academy to recommend me for the Accelerated Learning Program. The catch? No seats were available at Carney, so I'd have to attend Pulaski Elementary in the North End. My parents, siblings and anybody else that had something to say about it thought it was a phenomenal opportunity. I thought it was corny. All my friends were at Carney. This was going to suck.

First day of school: I'm nervous and pissed. I almost said FUCK THIS when I saw my classmates. It looked like a computer enthusiast summer camp. Out of 20 kids, 15 wore pocket protectors. I felt out of place. I'm from Westlawn. I was more comfortable around alcoholics and dope fiends than these kids. None of them did graffiti, no slang being spoken at lunch or recess, no breakdancing. A mess. To top it off, my boy Stevie told me they called my name for attendance in his class at Carney, and that class was full of all the wild, cool kids. I told him about my situation, and he just laughed. I had to get out of Pulaski.

One day, our school bus engine caught fire. We evacuated and waited for another bus. That was my excuse. I told my mom I was afraid to ride the bus. She wasn't having it. So, I went straight to the office the next day and told them I was no longer going to participate in the program. They called a parent meeting and tried talking me into staying. My being afraid of the bus story probably sounded crazy. But I held my ground. They signed me out. Mom dukes was vexed. CHECKMATE. Carney Academy, here I come.

Nowadays, I make a good living. No financial complaints. But I bust my ass all day. I bet those kids from Pulaski sit behind desks and make decisions. But I wanted to be a Hip-Hopping, Breakdancing, Slang Master B-Boy. (Said sarcastically.)

March 1987. I heard Criminal Minded first. The production was raw Bronx style—in your face BAM music. Very exoteric. No room for misunderstanding. KRS and Scott made a classic. But in July '87, everything I thought I knew about rhyme writing was flipped upside down and turned inside out. Kippy and Audra's younger sister, Regina, stayed at

The Great Solar Stance

the house for a weekend. When she left, she forgot her tapes. One of those cassettes was Paid in Full by Eric B. & Rakim.

The vocabulary alone had me sitting on the TV, watching the couch. Something about these words was magnetic. I didn't know anything about the Five % Nation. And still didn't after listening to this album over and over and over again. The phrases and concepts seemed so mathematical. Deciphering these crazy lyrics was fun to me.

Rakim's speech was like magic. I didn't understand the power even though I was pretending to. I was only eleven years old. At eleven, I could see the Kool Moe Dee two bar triple rhyme pattern was taken to another level. The whole project only had seven real songs. The other joints were DJ cuts and instrumentals. The poetry on those seven songs was out of this world. Science and Mathematics.

You already know that the new rhymes that I started writing had a different vocabulary than all my other verses that came before that album dropped. Rakim called himself God and I thought it was because of his skill level. I had no clue. Paid in Full held me down for the rest of '87.

Nate and I had some wild rhymes. At twelve and thirteen we rapped like superheroes. We wrote a lot. I can remember my first rhyme but can't remember any subsequent verses until a little before the Seven Headed Angel period. I wish I understood posterity and kept them all. That would've been a fly epilogue to this book.

Sky King

Rakim was a massive influence on my poetry around this time. Maybe too much. 1988 was coming. Not only was it the greatest year in rap music history, but it also brought the day that Tapski changed my life.

Chapter Five
1988

B-Boy music exploded in '88. Fly albums were coming out of everywhere—it was crazy. Sampling was creating an entirely new genre of beat production. Lyrics were both streetwise and intellectual. Rappers were conscious of who they were and who they were speaking to. You could feel the embodiment of the culture in almost every project that dropped.

Slick Rick - *The Great Adventures of Slick Rick*
Ultramagnetic MC's - *Critical Beatdown*
EPMD - *Strictly Business*
BDP - *By All Means Necessary*
Big Daddy Kane - *Long Live the Kane*
Public Enemy - *It Takes a Nation of Millions*
Eric B. & Rakim - *Follow the Leader*
MC Lyte - *Lyte as a Rock*
N.W.A - *Straight Outta Compton*
Ice-T – *Power*
Marley Marl - *In Control Volume 1*

Sky King

Biz Markie - *Goin' Off*
Eazy-E - *Eazy Duz It*
DJ Jazzy Jeff & the Fresh Prince - *He's the DJ, I'm the Rapper*
Stetsasonic - *In Full Gear*
Run DMC - *Tougher Than Leather*
Salt-N-Pepa - *A Salt with a Deadly Pepa*
Doug E. Fresh - *The World's Greatest Entertainer*
Kid 'n Play - *2 Hype*
Jungle Brothers - *Straight Out the Jungle*
Audio Two - *What More Can I Say?*
Super Lover Cee & Casanova Rud - *Girls I Got 'Em Locked*
Lakim Shabazz - *Pure Righteousness*
JVC Force - *Doin' Damage*

The very first episode of Yo! MTV Raps premiered in August 1988, hosted by Run DMC and DJ Jazzy Jeff & the Fresh Prince. I was at my grandmother's house with my radio pressed against the TV speaker so I could record the audio from the videos. *Follow the Leader* by Eric B. & Rakim was the first video Yo! MTV Raps ever played. I had no clue they had a new album on the way, and that was the first time I ever heard that song. Rakim kept his foot on the pedal. He took his poetry to the next level. I thought I was too—until I found out I wasn't.

One of my greatest hip-hop inspirations is my cousin Timmy Tap—a super B-Boy graffiti writer. Dude is just a walking source of slang, clothing, and overall style. I don't think I know another human personally with more knowledge of the culture than Tapski. That's for real. Whenever he would stop by the crib, he always had some innovation going on. After he left, I would always try to emulate his latest style. Tap is about eight years older than me. He was from the Ranch Crew out of the Potter Street projects.

One day, he came through while I was at the kitchen table writing. I was gassed. I figured this was my opportunity to impress him. To be validated by Tapski was a big deal for twelve-year-old Vernon. He already knew what I was doing. "Yo... what you doing, kid?" he asked. I told him I was writing rhymes. "Rhymes? Let me hear what you got."

I let that joint rip. BOOM! 12-gauge shotgun—highly potent lyrics to the grill. I was waiting for him to give me the kind of dap you give somebody when they do some unexpected, wild, amazing, classic shit. That dap never came.

My hip-hop hero looked at me all serious and said, "That shit was wack. You sound like a fake Rakim. You're a biter." My smile turned upside down. He called me a biter. I got a sudden case of the bubble guts. I was completely devastated. It felt like I was having a heart attack. I almost cried—no bullshit.

He told me that if I was going to be an emcee, I had to be original. I had to be Vernon. I couldn't be Rakim. There already was a Rakim, and he was better than I was. He gave me regular dap, then he broke out.

I threw that verse in the fucking garbage. I didn't even tell Nate about that cataclysmic event. I was embarrassed. But when all that "woe is me" stuff finally wore off, I was determined to make Tap a believer. I was a believer. I knew I was an emcee. Tap's advice went a long way. That brutal honesty is what an artist needs to set them on the right path. It didn't hinder me—it reinforced my dedication and devotion to the craft.

All praise is due to Tap. He could've easily done some sucker shit and had me thinking one thing while reality said another. I've witnessed Tap drop the axe on another emcee's neck. I was a grown-ass man at the time, and that shit was tough to watch. It's not pretty, but it's necessary. You've got to respect the truth. I had to dig deep to find Vernon the emcee. The universe was about to show me what it meant to be an MC—as in Move the Crowd.

My cousin Derek and I went to the Future Stars '88 Talent Show at New Bedford High School. We got there early, so we people watched and laughed as the auditorium filled up. We were sitting next to the left aisle, so when the Potter Street dudes came in, they rolled right by us. Ju Ju Platt led the way with the illest strut I had ever seen. The vision of that walk was seared into my memory. I mean that strut was HARDCORE. He had his Ranch Crew hat tilted to the side. The visual was crazy B-Boy.

There were a lot of acts that night—live bands, rap groups, lip-syncers, and dancers. A local beat maker named Beat Box Paul had a hand in four or five of the performances.

The Great Solar Stance

One of those groups was a rap crew called Tuff Enuff. Ant from Westlawn was the emcee, Earl and Billy were the dancers, and Dwayne Branco was the DJ. I'm not sure what his DJ name was back then, but later, he would transform into DJ Rareform. Paul played the beat from a keyboard and sang the hook on one of their tracks. They performed a song called "Style," and when the hook dropped, the lights flashed in time with the beat. It was a well-put-together show. Tuff Enuff got busy that night.

But for me, the moment that blew my wig clean off was when Tito & The Rock performed their version of "It Takes Two." Tito and my man B-Boy Sane crushed the entire talent show. Dave Conceicao and Curt Cruz were doing the James Brown dance flawlessly all over the stage. Sane had the drum pattern rocking, and they commanded the crowd's attention. The whole auditorium was out of their seats, dancing. That's my word. They owned the stage—left, right, center—moving with massive confidence like it was effortless. It looked easy for them. That was the first time I truly understood the meaning of being an MC and the importance of a solid performance. Everything was coming together for me. I was seeing all the different elements of the art form, and I knew I had to make my vision a reality. I just needed to bake the cake. My vision had to be manifested. I wanted to do a show. I wanted to perform. But deep down, I still felt like a little kid—like I wouldn't be taken seriously.

Sky King

During the '88-'89 school year, I was in junior high, and my little cousin TJ came to live with us. His father, Tommy, is my mother's brother. After TJ's mom passed away, he first lived with his grandmother in the Potter Street projects, but since we had plenty of room on Sycamore Street, my mom took him in. I was about thirteen, and he was around ten. Since I was the youngest of my mother's and father's children, it was cool having a little brother.

At the time, Nate was a freshman in high school. Derek and I would meet up in the morning, pick up Taj, and walk to school. I was still close with Nate, but I spent a lot of time with Silk (Derek) and started running with Taj, too. Nate was doing his own thing—he was an athlete, and he had that camaraderie with the sports squad. And Nate was no joke on the football field—he'd run you right over. For a kid with a smaller stature, he was strong as hell. Don't sleep on him. He was a quiet dude, but he had hands. If you got out of line, you were getting your ass beat.

One day, Nate told me he had been rocking with this youth action group at the Boys Club called TWT (Teens with Talent). He'd been running with Tyrone and Jason from the Club, and both were in TWT. When I first heard "Teens with Talent," I thought it was about talent shows and performing arts. I was hyped, I wanted in. But then I found out it stood for Teens Working Together. SIKE! Nate was really in it because there were some girls from the South End affiliated with the group. It made sense to me, so I joined.

The Great Solar Stance

I already knew Tyrone and Jason. Tyrone lived on the Hillman Street side of Westlawn, and Jason lived at the top of Maxfield St. Both were tight with my cousin Cory, so we were all familiar. Jason had a fly crib, and it became our rally point, especially in the summer. He had a pool with a plastic dome, so the water stayed warm. Some dudes would show up at his door in swim trunks with a towel around their neck like, "What's up, Jay? What are you doing today? It's hot out."

One day, we were in Jason's room playing music when I just came out and told them that Nate and I rhymed. Naturally, they wanted to hear some. We dropped our verses, and they were digging it. We talked about starting a crew. Tyrone said he could be the DJ— he had a Sound Design single-component turntable stereo with a handful of records. Jason said he and Cory could be the dancers. In '89, most rappers had dancers for live shows. Nate and I were down.

We didn't have a name yet, and it took a while to come up with one. Then we met this kid named Josh, who had just moved in across from Nate. He told us he rhymed and that his dad had some beat-making equipment. His dad lived a few blocks away, so we rolled over there, eager to get busy.

None of us had any experience making beats or knew how to use the equipment. Josh's dad wasn't home, so we opened a window and went in. His dad had a small studio apartment in some rooming house on Campbell Street, one room with a bathroom and a kitchenette. We started snooping through his stuff and found his porno magazines. His place was a mess.

Sky King

But Josh wasn't lying—his dad really had equipment: a TR505 drum machine, two keyboards, and a tape deck. We couldn't figure out how to program the drum machine, so two of us tapped out the drums live. Jason came up with a whistle-type melody on the keyboard. Then we found a cassette with some of Josh's dad's music on it. His band's sound was all over the place—crazy wild and erratic. We were like, "Fuck this wack shit," and recorded our beat right over his father's music—zero hesitation. Josh didn't even care.

I still remember Jason's melody, and occasionally, I play it for nostalgia's sake. Our beat was nuts. Since we played it live, the tempo kept speeding up and slowing down. One of us hit the kick and snare while another tapped the hi-hat. Jason played the keys. We recorded that beat for like five minutes. I wish I still had that recording.

We left the apartment and went straight to Jason's room to play our beat. That joint got mad burn—it was on heavy rotation. Josh claimed he rhymed, but none of us had ever heard him spit. One time, we all went to his spot in the Lawn to write a joint. Nate and I wrote our verses and spit them. Josh took forever to write his verse. When he finally did, he straight-up recited a KRS-One verse from "Criminal Minded." Like we weren't hip to BDP in '87? We knew right then he was tripping—he couldn't get down with us musically.

One time we saw Josh coming down Maxfield Street. As we got closer, he reached into his pocket, fidgeted, and suddenly his beeper began to beep. He pulled it out like he was important enough to be paged—except we saw him trigger the beep himself. He was a mess. Years later, I linked up with Josh on Facebook just before he passed away. May the universe be pleased with Josh.

Chapter Six
Duane Darock

Positively Youth was another teen organization in New Bedford. They threw parties at the Y.W.C.A. once a month, which we called "Y" parties. These were the spot back then—eighteen-and-under jump-offs. All the young females from every side of the city would be there. At the end of the night, they'd play a slow jam, and you could find yourself a nice little shorty, hug up on her, be all in her neck, and squeeze on her bum. That was the move.

It was at one of these Y parties that Jason connected the dots. He had this fake gold bracelet we used to wear across our fingers like a four-finger ring. It was always lying around his bedroom. After one of the parties, I was outside the Y on Spring Street talking to some girls when Jason came over and told me he had given Darock the bracelet in exchange for making some beats for us. That was a major power move. Darock was the most prominent rapper in New B at the time—he had a manager, a producer, and was getting paid for shows. He was known for rhyming off the top of his head—

The Great Solar Stance

spontaneous, unwritten rhymes. Jason got his number, and Darock told us to call him the next day to set something up.

We called, set up an appointment, and showed up at his crib at the designated time. Darock lived in Harbor View Towers, across the street from Bay Village Projects. Nate, Tyrone, and I made the trip. Turns out, Darock and Tyrone were family. We rang the buzzer, and he told us to come up. At that moment, it felt real—I had half expected him not to be there. But he answered the door, introduced us to his mom, and led us to his room. I remember seeing Word Up! magazine pages of Big Daddy Kane and Rakim on his wall. That was common— most young hip-hoppers had their favorite rapper's Word Up! pics scotch-taped to their bedroom walls.

Darock had a Casio SK-5 keyboard. Unlike the SK-1, which could only hold one sample, the SK-5 could store two, with each sample maxing out at two seconds. What he did with that keyboard was ingenious. He set up his double cassette tape deck to record at high speed. The play deck had a drum break from Soul Makossa, and the record deck was set up with the pause button engaged. He ran a wire from the "headphone out" port of the tape deck to the "line in" port on the Casio. When he pressed play, the Soul Makossa drums played at high speed (2.5x). He hit the sample button on the downbeat, capturing the entire loop in under two seconds. When the loop was played back, it was played at a lower key, restoring it to its original tempo. Voila! A workaround for the sample time constraint.

Sky King

I had the same keyboard and had never even thought of that technique—hadn't even considered using it to make beats. He used the same trick to sample a guitar. Once he had the samples he wanted, he looped the drums and played the guitar sample manually over them. He recorded that onto a tape, erased the samples, and then sampled a ghostly-sounding synth. Then, he played back the first tape with the drums and guitar while adding the synth live—recording the whole thing onto another tape. And just like that, we had our first original beat. I can't lie—that joint came out dope. Darock came through for us.

We took the beat home, and Nate and I wrote a song called *You'll Get Taken*—our first real joint. Tyrone was going to scratch Eazy-E saying "You'll get taken" from *Straight Outta Compton* for the hook.

Now, let me backtrack quickly. When we were in Jason's room deciding to form a crew, I don't think Tyrone had given any real thought to being a DJ before that moment. But it made sense—he was the only one with records and a turntable stereo. By then, Kippy had his own spot, so I no longer had access to equipment. It seemed like as soon as he decided to be a DJ, he instantly learned how to scratch—no joke. We even modified the volume slider on his stereo to simulate a mixer crossfader, using a piece of a box fan grate to minimize the distance from zero to half-max loudness. He started transforming and doing all types of cuts. It was meant to be.

The Great Solar Stance

Now, back to our new joint. We had the beat, the lyrics, and the cuts. I'm not sure if we ever thought about recording it— we wanted to perform it. Neither of us had code names at the time. Tap always called me V-Neck, so I ran with V-Nek. Tyrone became T-Rek, and I think Nate just stuck with Nate— he wasn't into all the extra bullshit. One thing we didn't have. A name for the group.

Chapter Seven
The Show

I saw a flyer about a talent show at Keith Jr. High School. This was exactly what I had been waiting for. The show was being organized by Manny Carter—host of MCTV, a TV show on the public access channel. The crazy thing is we found out that Manny was Josh's father. Now, we had a face to go along with the studio apartment we had violated. Now, we knew who owned all those lame porno magazines with the ugly women.

Mr. Carter was always downtown filming his show. His right-hand man was a dude who played in his band. I can't remember his name, but he had a wild, nappy beard with no mustache. That thing almost touched his chest hair. Nate joked that his beard looked like it was crawling down his neck. Nate always had the best observations. Then, he started calling him Abe Lincoln, and from that point on, we all referred to him as Abe Lincoln. I wonder where that guy is now. I wonder if he still has that beard.

Anyway, we couldn't sign up for the show without a name, so we started brainstorming. One day, Nate and I were

The Great Solar Stance

listening to *I Ain't No Joke* by Rakim, and when he said, "Guide you out of triple stage darkness," we looked at each other like, Yooooo!!!! That's it right there—Triple Stage Darkness. We had no idea what it meant. There weren't any Gods in New Bedford at that time spreading knowledge of self. We just thought it sounded dope. Everyone agreed on the name, and just like that, it was official. Little did we know, we were calling ourselves Blind, Deaf, and Dumb. When you play stupid games, you win stupid prizes. Years later, when I was exposed to the Nation of Gods and Earths and the 5 Percent teachings, this situation was one of the first things that came to mind.

We signed up for the show, so now we need to practice. My cousin Robby Mendes at the Boys' Club let us use a room upstairs to rehearse. We were in there every day after school, putting in work. Jason and Cory came up with a dance routine, and we made sure our performance was tight. I had never rocked in public before, but I wanted it so bad that I wasn't even scared. The only part that felt weird was performing in front of our parents. I was only about fourteen at the time, so my mom was coming to this. All our moms came through for this one.

One of the other groups in the show was Definitely Smooth. These kids were the sons of one of the members of the legendary R&B group Tavares. They were on some Bell Biv DeVoe, Dallas Austin type vibe—but with Hammer pants and patent leather shoes. We knew that going up against singers was an uphill battle, but I didn't care about winning. I just wanted to rock the stage.

I didn't even know what I was going to wear. Nate had these blue Nike sweatpants that looked like a Nike sweatsuit my brother Boo had. His suit was the same shade of blue too. Word! That's what we were going to rock. The day before the show, I asked Boo if I could wear his suit, and this chump told me NO. I was pissed. Started calling him all kinds of names. How is he not going to let me get busy in the suit? Doesn't he know how important this is? I couldn't believe it. After I called him a sucker a few times, he said I was NOT wearing it. I was on some fuck him type shit.

I knew I was wearing that fucking suit. This was my first show, and it was going down the right way.

SHOWTIME. You already know what I did. Went right in his room, took the suit, and snatched his brand-new gray-on-white hi-top Air Force STS's. I was not playing. The universe works in mysterious ways. Nate only had Nike pants, but Donny Livramento happened to be backstage wearing the exact same Nike jacket I had on. What are the fucking chances of that? Unbelievable. We asked him if Nate could rock the coat, and he was with it. Everything was coming together.

A woman introduced us, and Triple Stage Darkness took the stage for the first time. I looked at the crowd and got the bubble guts. But when it was go time, I shook that shit off and dove in. It went down like a cold glass of water. No mistakes. I would pay a ton of money to see footage of that show.

The Great Solar Stance

Manny Carter introduced Definitely Smooth, but when he said their name, he pronounced it "Debonibidy Smoov." We laughed about that for years. Anytime someone in the squad mentioned Manny Carter, someone would always say, "Debonibidy Smoov." They performed on a few MCTV shows, and every time he introduced them, it was "Debonibidy Smoov."

When those Tavares kids hit the stage, they came out like gangbusters. Nate had said something hilarious—I can't remember what it was, but I just remember us all cracking up. Their performance was crazy up-tempo, full of all the latest dance moves. I.O.U. sweaters galore. All the little shorties in the crowd were hyped.

We knew we had lost this one. Rap was not beating R&B. They won first place in every talent show they entered. We rocked about three or four shows with them, and we always came in second place. We might've done You'll Get Taken in every show. LMAO.

Chapter Eight
Beat Box Paul

Nate began to excel in football and started focusing on his post–high school life. Rap music wasn't a priority for him. Tyrone and I had different plans. We started crate digging—scavenging for old records to find samples for beats.

Tyrone moved out of Westlawn and relocated to Mill Street, about two blocks away from the Lawn. He lived on the first floor, while Foo Foo and Rob Dog lived on the second. Foo used to snatch Tyrone's wife beaters from the clothesline in the backyard. Foo Foo had also moved there from Westlawn; they used to live directly across from Nate.

We would sit in Tyrone's room and loop samples on that Casio SK-5. One day, I ran into my man RJ and asked him for his brother's phone number. RJ's brother is Beat Box Paul. I knew RJ from the Lawn—he used to do head spins on the cement walkways. No cardboard. Straight dome piece on cement.

We called Paul and scheduled a session. He charged ten dollars an hour for beats. Paul had the fly beat style, anyone

The Great Solar Stance

rhyming at the time wanted to rock with him. He lived around the corner from the Potter Street projects. Tyrone and I walked there with the records we wanted to sample. One of them was a James Brown joint from the *Black Caesar* soundtrack.

Paul's setup was in the basement. He had a sampling keyboard workstation called an Ensoniq EPS. I had no idea how much that keyboard would eventually impact my life. Paul went to work on that joint, and I was fascinated. He was pressing all kinds of buttons crazy fast—looping samples, creating a hook, putting different sequences together, and arranging them into a full song. He moved so quickly I couldn't follow. After watching him, I knew I wanted that knowledge.

Paul told us someone had stolen the EPS and sold it to him, but it didn't come with an instruction manual. He had to figure it out on his own.

We ended up recording two joints at Paul's spot— one about me smashing all kinds of girls, and the other just some wild, hard, battle-rhyme type shit.

While Tyrone and I were trying to get things popping, another rhyme squad was also going to Beat Box Paul for beats. Private Stock consisted of Sabu, Aaron, Ricky, and Wayne. I didn't know Sabu well, but I knew who he was. I went to elementary school with Aaron and Ricky. I knew of Wayne because he was sort of famous for being a fly dancer. These cats used to get busy on some serious B-Boy status—pure, energetic Hip-Hop.

Sky King

The Standard Times, the local newspaper, even wrote an article on Private Stock and Manny Carter. They were making noise in the New Bedford rap scene, and we slowly started connecting here and there.

Cory moved to Chancery Street and started linking up with Stevie, who had transformed into Spank, and Michael Pina. Michael lived on Spruce St. across from Ricky. I'd known Spank since early Carney Academy days, but we never ran together. Now we were hanging out frequently. Spank was already down with the Private Stock cats, and I believe he and Ricky were tight through the Spruce Street crew. Eventually, Ricky started hanging at Jason's house now and then, and one day, he brought a reluctant Wayne over.

After meeting Wayne I could tell he didn't give a fuck about chilling with some new dudes, but he was cool about it. Right away, I could see he was a shoe enthusiast like me. I also got the vibe that he didn't like me. Neither of us knew then how tight we would eventually become—or that for the next thirty-something years, we'd be locked in a secret footwear battle.

Chapter Nine
DJ Super V

Ricky, whose rhyme name was P-Nut, made a solo track called Sampling Psychology. We used to joke about him reading the dictionary, looking for words that rhymed. The first time I heard that song was at Ricky's house. His place had more food than any other house I had ever been in—snacks galore on every counter, closets filled with canned goods and non-perishable packages. He was crazy generous with the treats. You could have anything. As soon as you walk in, he'd offer all kinds of snacks.

I assumed he recorded the song at Paul's spot, but I never asked. It was a dope joint with its own unique style—had a Deee-Lite type of vibe. A few weeks later, Ricky calls me and says I must go with him to DJ Super V's house. He wanted me to check out Super V's setup.

I asked, "What kind of sampler does he use? Ricky said, "He doesn't have a sampler. He uses his turntables." I was totally confused. My brother had turntables, and I couldn't understand how someone could make beats with them. Then

Ricky played me his new song, *Cock Diesel*, he told me it was produced by Super V.

I was steamrolled. That track blew my eyebrows off. I was fucking impressed. Out of all the songs us local dudes were making at that time; Cock Diesel was top of the food chain. That track single-handedly shifted me into gear and made me focus on being serious. After hearing it, there was no question—I was going to Super V's crib. I had to know how he was doing what he did.

Ricky and I walked to his spot on Bay Street. I had never met Super V before that day. I figured he was Black. Turns out, he was a nerdy-looking Portuguese kid. Taking him at face value was a major mistake. Super V was ultra B-Boy from the Bronx. A ridiculous Hip-Hop historian, with all the cassettes to prove it. He had recordings from the '70s—cases filled with party tapes of live sets from the Cold Crush Brothers, Fantastic Freaks, The L Brothers, and more. I couldn't believe it.

Then he showed me how his setup worked. Super V—real name Victor—used a four-track tape recorder to layer breaks and samples. Just like a DJ extends breaks with two turntables, he used the four-track to extend a drum beat on two of the four tracks. Then, he'd bounce those two tracks down to one, leaving three tracks open. Instead of sampling the usual way, he cut samples live on the turntables over the drumbeat, repeating the process of bouncing and layering.

Victor came up with some real fly production. He let me hear a snippet of the mixtape he was working on, and once

The Great Solar Stance

again, he tore the fabric of the space-time continuum. He raised the bar way beyond my imagination. THIS was what a mixtape was supposed to sound like.

He never just played a song—there was no beginning and no end. It was one continuous blend of breakbeats, songs, acapellas, and soundscapes, all layered together. I couldn't wait for that tape to drop. Vic gave me a copy to show Tyrone. I knew his dome was going to mushroom cloud when he peeped this.

I'm not sure he would be the DJ he is today without the inspiration and innovation of DJ Super V. Tyrone had turntables now—I forgot how he got them, but he got them. And when he found out about the Fostex four track, he went on a mission to get one.

One day at his crib, while we were playing music, he put on The Biz Never Sleeps by Biz Markie. Even though we'd heard that album hundreds of times, we all froze when we heard: "Hey Mudfoot, you know what we're here for. Lay some treats on us." The famous Mudfoot scene from Fat Albert.

Everybody was thinking the same thing. That was his new name. And on that day, Tyrone transformed into DJ Mudfoot.

Chapter Ten
The Four Track

Mud gets a Fostex four-track, and everything starts changing. All the loops we make on the Casio SK-5 are now getting dumped onto the four-track. The keyboard doesn't have a memory card, so we can't save any loops—once you shut it off, that's it. You lose all the samples. Now we're storing them on tapes.

We need a microphone. We ran into Mud's grandmother at the mall, and he asked her for ten dollars so we could buy one from Radio Shack. Agnes Quarles comes through for us. This was the beginning of our off-the-head rhyme training. We spent hours upon hours in Mud's room, doming over our loops. No songs were getting recorded—just us going off the top. Even dudes who didn't usually rhyme would jump in on a beat. We used to have mad fun at Mud's crib.

Mud showed me a joint that Aaron and Sabu had laced over a beat that we put together. I was writing to it at the time. Aaron was A-Dog, and Sabu was 40oz Bu. The very first lines of the first verse were: "UHHMM... Let me clear my esophagus, 40 Bu gets stupid while shooting out more ink than an octopus." Then he blacks out and leaves Earth. Aaron comes in and starts his verse the same way but with different words—and he fucking manhandles the rest of the beat. After hearing that, I didn't want to write to that loop anymore. They owned it now.

At that moment, I wanted to be in Private Stock. After hearing Ricky's Cock Deez joint and what these cats just did to my loop, I knew these were the gods. I sat in my room for almost an entire weekend, trying to write the flyest rhymes I could muster up. Straight writer's block. I couldn't come up with anything I felt was on their level. I wanted to present them with some dope shit so I could get down, but the universe wasn't on my team. It wasn't meant to be.

Still, I knew I had it in me to rock shit—I just had to keep being me instead of trying to ride their wave. Mud and I were putting some fresh ideas together, but we were limited by the Casio. Mud started working on his own mixtape. Now I had the Casio at my house, sampling all kinds of shit. But without a four-track to record the loops, I was basically just practicing. Practice makes perfect.

I still didn't think of myself as a beatmaker. I was an emcee. Beat Box Paul and Darock had moved to California, and I didn't know anybody else in New B making fly beats. I don't even remember why we stopped going to Super V's house. We were on our own. It was probably early '91 by this time. Enter my man, Duane Barboza.

Sky King

I had known Duane since kindergarten. Carney Academy had a lot of future B-Boys back in the early 1980s. Duane was in a few of my high school classes, and one day, he brought in a tape of some of his beats. He didn't sample—he made his joints with keyboards and guitars. His production style was crazy fly. I picked out a beat and wrote a song called *Smooth with the Rufness*.

Duane lived across the street from New Bedford High, so I went to his spot after school to record my verses. He was also a DJ—he could make beats and scratch. Back in junior high, his name was DJ Demolish, but I can't remember if he kept it.

I wanted him to cut "Smooth with the roughness" from the Poor Righteous Teachers song *Rock Dis Funky Joint* for this new track, but he didn't have that record. I knew Mud had it. I called his house, but he wasn't there. I tracked him down somehow and asked him to call his mother, so she'd let me in to grab the record. He was sort of salty about that—and I get it. He was my DJ. He must've been thinking, "What kind of sucker shit is this?" I had no ill intentions, and I think he knew that.

Duane produced the track, so it was like how DJ Premier did cuts for Lord Finesse, even though Finesse had DJ Mike Smooth. Duane came through on the scratches, and the song came out dope. We played it on WSMU 91.1. Whenever somebody in the area made a new joint, they played it on the Heather Landers Show— Sunday nights from 8 to 11.

The Great Solar Stance

I thought Duane and I were going to make a lot of joints together. Then he told me he rhymed too and was going to rock some of the beats he had played for me. I had zero problem with that—those were his beats.

He told me he was heading to 91.1 to play one of his new songs, so I tuned in that night. When his song came on, it melted my face off. I couldn't believe what I was hearing. It was one of the beats he had shown me, but the rhyme wasn't his.

He had really spit Positive K's verse from *A Good Combination*. Maybe he thought nobody had ever heard that Positive K joint before. Maybe he figured people forgot about it. I really don't know. I never asked him.

But I took the B-Boy stance seriously. That Solar Stance—that Great Solar Stance—was everything my brother instilled in me. After that, I felt a certain way about making music with Duane. So, I just let it fade off.

He was still my man, though. We stayed mad cool— we just didn't make any more music. May the Universe be pleased with Duane Barboza.

Chapter Eleven
Law School

I'm in tenth grade, and Ricky is in a few of my classes. He was a wild cowboy. One time, he told our geography teacher that he was going to take his wife and smash her. The teacher said, "Excuse me?" Ricky replied, "You heard me. I'll pull your wife." All the kids were cracking up.

Ricky was also in my Spanish class. He and I got into a lot of shit together. We used to hustle hard between classes. From the moment I walked into school each day, I'd start asking people for fifty cents. I did this all day long. We'd skip whatever class we had during lunch period and stay through all three lunch shifts, just hustling. I would hit up all the females—White, Black, Spanish, and Portuguese. They all knew the deal. Most girls would give me dollars, sometimes fives.

Both of us were getting way out of hand. One day, I racked up eighty-two dollars and fifty cents. I don't remember how much Ricky got that day, but I do remember that we left school, got on a bus to Boston, and bought some kicks.

The Great Solar Stance

Later, in Spanish class, Ricky and I were talking about our financial power moves when our teacher, Ms. Pearson, overheard us. She turned us in to the Gold Housemaster, Mr. Longo. At New Bedford High, the student population was divided into four houses—Green, Gold, Tan, and Blue. Ricky and I were both in Gold.

Ms. Pearson told Mr. Longo that we were extorting students for money. By the time we finished pleading our case, the only thing Mr. Longo had left to say was, "You guys should go to law school. Now get out of my office and stop asking kids for money." Ms. Pearson was pissed—she wanted us to be punished.

Ricky, though, leveled up. He started linking up with a girl who gave him hundreds of dollars a day—no bullshit. His gear catalog was up. His shoe game was up. He was shining. He would walk through the halls of New Bedford High with drink boxes that matched his clothes. He wasn't playing. He even took me to Boston after school a few times.

While sitting in Spanish class, he said, "Yo, me and you should be a crew. You know, rhyme together." I was with it. We started making it happen.

Manny Carter put on a show at the library downtown. A stage was set up right in front of the main steps. It was packed. Ricky and I practiced and practiced. We had our routine on smash—or so we thought.

When it was time for us to rock, we started our little crowd participation act. But when I was supposed to start rhyming, I forgot the first word of my verse. I just started saying gibberish—no real words at all, just sounds to the rhythm of the beat. Thank God the sound system was terrible—it masked what was really going on. Nobody knew I was talking nonsense. Ricky knew, though. He was bugging out.

But here's the crazy part—when Ricky started his verse, he forgot his shit too. So, he did the same thing I did. And the crowd loved us.

We got off stage, and my man Jonathan Ribeiro came up to me and said, "You cats are dope. You guys sound like a young Kool G Rap." That shit was crazy. We didn't say a legit word, but people were showing us love, saying we killed that show.

Tenth grade was a good year for me. That's when I realized how dope Sabu was with the lyrics.

I was sitting in study hall when this girl passed me a note saying she wanted to link up with me. The note also said her sister wanted to hook up with Sabu. I caught up with Bu and let him know the scoop. We set it up to meet them at Bu's crib after school.

Bu and I stopped at my house first, then headed straight up Sycamore Street to Spruce. Bu and Wayne lived together on Spruce Street. It's crazy how Spruce Street played such a significant role in my life.

On the way to his crib, Bu let off a rhyme. His words were on some exotic-type shit. As he recited each bar, I was

The Great Solar Stance

thinking, What the fuck is he gonna rhyme with that? Dude was better than emcees who were on records. That was the moment Bu Ruk became my favorite emcee.

Sabu was Rakim, Kane, Grand Puba, Slick Rick, and the entire year of 1988 all rolled into one. I wish I could remember that verse. After hearing that, I didn't give a fuck about those two shorties. I wanted to make music.

They came to the crib, and homegirl was all over me, but all I could think about was samples and beats. Shit was crazy. I just wanted to get to my little Casio keyboard and whip something up.

Chapter Twelve
Basics Of Organized Knowledge

Eleventh grade was when I decided to start preparing for college. In elementary school, I took education seriously. But when I got to junior high, that all changed. Girls were paying attention to me, and they were down to get busy. I didn't give a fuck about books or homework.

I messed up in seventh and eighth grades so bad that I had to go to summer school just to graduate from junior high school. I wasn't trying to stay back, so I went. But my dumb ass still played around and got shitty grades in ninth and tenth. High school had way too many females. They came from all over the city, and a lot of them were giving me rhythm. It was easy to get sidetracked.

But when eleventh grade started in 1991, I knew it was time to get back on track. I selected all college-level courses, and they were too easy for me—I was blowing through with straight A's.

Then, my first child was born in November of my junior year. I was fifteen years old. LeRynn Rakell Gilmette arrived

The Great Solar Stance

on November 27, 1991. I got a few bullshit after-school jobs, but they never lasted long. Even with a newborn, my momentum never slowed. I kept an A average in most of my classes, maybe a B+ in one or two.

That's when I heard about a group in school called Talent Search. Once again, I thought it was about talent, but it wasn't. Students could go to the Talent Search room instead of study hall, where my man Gil Carlisle would educate us on the many post-high school opportunities out there. That's where I discovered Five Towns College in New York—a music school in Dix Hills, Long Island. My plan was to ace the SATs, get accepted, and move to NYC.

In January of '92, the movie Juice came out. Ricky decided he was going to turn the city upside down. He started wildin' out—armed robberies and all types of shit. He was getting money, but he got bagged up. That put our music on pause.

Wayne and I were walking out of school when he told me he was changing his name. He had gone by Boogieman during the P-Stock days—Wayne is no joke when it comes to dancing. The man can boogie. He's also a fashion innovator. At first, I thought he was just changing Boogieman, but nah—he was now Saadiq Abdul Aziz. "Don't call me Wayne anymore, that's not my name" he said. And at that moment, right in front of my eyes, Wayne transformed into Saadiq.

Chapter Thirteen
Tim Fim

Somehow, Spank and I got our hands on a keyboard. I can't remember who let me hold it, but we were standing on the corner of Park and Kempton, using the payphone, with that bullshit Radio Shack piano under my arm. Guess who walks up on us? Motherfucking Tapski comes out of nowhere, starts laughing, and says, "What are you niggas doing with that piece of shit?" I told him I was going to make some beats. He said, "Not with that. I'm gonna take you to my man Fim's crib. He got the official keyboard." Tap called Fim, who said we could come through. Fim lived in Fairhaven, so we trooped over the bridge to his spot.

Spank was already close with Fim, whose real name was Timmy Pina, older brother to Michael Pina from the Spruce Street crew. Tim "Fim" was a super-duper B-Boy, graff writer, DJ, and producer. He was down with the Ranch crew and TSP, and his tag was Spy. Fim was no joke. When we got to Fim's, he had an Ensoniq EPS Plus. I mentioned I'd been going to Paul's spot for beats and that Paul had the same keyboard, but

The Great Solar Stance

Fim already knew. He said he was close with Paul's whole family—even appearing in one of their family photos. It's crazy how everyone in my journey was connected.

Fim asked me what I was looking for, and I just said, "beats." I told him I wanted to learn to make beats myself, so he showed me some of his work. I picked out three beats, and he began teaching me how to use the EPS. He gave me his number and invited me to come by whenever, but insisted I had to be consistent. Fim didn't play around or tolerate fronting. This was exactly what I'd been waiting for—hands-on training.

He helped me put together numerous beats. Mud and I were crate-digging like champions, bringing ideas to Fim, who'd put his special touch on them. We made some fly shit. There was one particularly intricate joint, featuring drums, a bassline sample, horns, and a four-bar chorus sample. The four-bar sample veered off-beat, but somehow Fim broke it up and placed it perfectly, arranging the sequences into song mode. I knew this was going to be the one that would make the Private Stock cats recognize that I'd arrived. I wanted them to feel the way I felt when I heard their music.

I took that beat home and wrote a joint called "*Stick-up Kid*," my first storytelling rhyme. Mud scratched the hook—"blew off his top when the pistol went pop" from Kool G Rap's *Road to the Riches*. The bridge used a different beat, and we slowed our voices to sound like dudes plotting to kill the stick-up kid. This track was bananas. We utilized every trick his four-track had. Mud and I were amped when we finished recording; I had the bubble guts, eager to show it off.

Ricky lived with my cousin Cerrie in Presidential Heights Projects, which everybody called Presi (prezee). When I called the crib, Ricky said he was there with Saadiq, Aaron, and Sabu. The universe was on my side— it was the perfect time to unveil this joint.

When we walked in, everyone was in the kitchen at the table. The radio was ready. I entered quoting Cholly from Beat Street, "I got a rocket in my pocket," but nobody caught the reference. I pulled the tape from my pocket, popped it into the deck, and pressed play. When the joint ended, everyone was bugging out, like, "What the fuck was that?" Their reactions told me I'd returned the favor—they felt what I felt hearing Ricky's joint, experiencing the same excitement. They felt what I felt when I heard Bu and Aaron rock my loop. Aaron asked, "Who made that?" I said Mud and I did. The cuts on that joint were razor sharp. Aaron said, "Yo, nigga, we're rocking with you!"

I didn't create a new name that day, but I transformed into a better artist. My confidence soared. I told them we'd made the track at Tim Fim's spot, suggesting we should start going there regularly. However, there was an issue: apparently, Fim had beef with their cousin Hakim and had stabbed him. Aaron didn't care, laughing and saying, "Nigga, I'm trying to make these joints." Saadiq was open to discussing it with Fim but

The Great Solar Stance

wouldn't commit, while Bu was firmly against it, refusing outright to go to Fim's crib.

Mud and I continued going to Fim's to produce beats and record them on his four-track. Fim patiently walked me through every step of using the EPS. He was genuinely trying to teach me everything he knew about the workstation. I desperately wanted an EPS of my own. Eventually, something changed in Fim's living situation, and we lost touch for a while. Rest in peace, Timmy Pina. May the Universe be pleased with him.

Chapter Fourteen
Five Towns College

My senior year in high school was easy. I focused on my grades and scoring high on the SATs so I could get into Five Towns. Gil was no longer with Talent Search, but another gentleman named Mike replaced him. Mike was cool as shit—he vouched for students and got them out of jams with their housemasters.

I took the SAT and scored 1340. That test is way too long. I started getting anxious, and I couldn't sit still. Anybody who knows me knows I have zero patience. Mike helped me with my application to Five Towns, and we got the ball rolling. Now we played the waiting game.

Twelfth grade was when I found my love for reading. During astronomy class, I was sitting in the planetarium when I glanced back at a classmate named Darren, who was reading a novel—*The Gunslinger* by Stephen King. Darren was a cool kid, kind of nerdy. Since I was a closet nerd myself, he was alright with me. He started explaining the plot of the seven-book series, and I was intrigued. After school, I went to Waldenbooks in the mall and bought the first three books. I

The Great Solar Stance

read the first one but didn't dive into the others because I was too busy doing dumb shit. I did a lot of dumb shit when I was young.

We used to love driving around in stolen cars. One night, I was chilling at Mud's crib, messing around with some electric racecars, when my cousin TJ called. He said he had a Nissan Stanza and was coming to scoop us up. My daughter's mother wanted me to slide through so we could get sexy, but I told her I had something to do.

TJ pulled up with my man Doug from the Lawn. Mud and I got in, and we headed to Fairhaven to see a girl TJ was messing with. Her best friend was there, and a week or so before, TJ had gotten into it with her and punched her in the face. Homegirl wasn't going out like that, so when we left, she called the cops and told them we were in a stolen car.

I was driving when we left the house. As soon as we got onto Route 6, the jakes was on our tail. I gunned it, flying down Route 6—all green lights. I couldn't believe it. Every single light was green.

We crossed the Fairhaven bridge and were about to go over the overpass when TJ looked at me and said, "V, this car got no brakes!" Whaaaaat??? Oh shiiiiiiit!! We smashed into the wall of the overpass. I thought we were going to blast right through it and crash-land onto Route 18. The only image I remember seeing was LeRynn's face. I really thought we were all dying that night.

Sky King

After hitting the wall, we crashed into a few cop cars. When I realized I wasn't dead, I opened the door and started running. I got about ten feet before I heard, "V, don't leave me!" It was TJ. I turned around, ran back, grabbed him, and we jetted—hopped over the wall and ran down the hill to Route 18.

Route 18 has three lanes on each side. We did some Frogger-type shit, dodging cars as we crossed the entire highway. I didn't see Mud or Doug when I got out of the car, but as soon as TJ and I made it across, we heard Mud screaming for the cops. "Five-Oh! Five-Oh! Help me!!!" I couldn't see him, but I could hear him. TJ and I thought the jakes were fucking him up.

We ran to Metro Medic at the bottom of Maxfield Street, busted a move, and hid in my cousin Cory Pina's hallway for about 45 minutes. The street was quiet, so we jetted back to our crib on Sycamore Street. It had to be after midnight when we got home.

At around 2 a.m., the phone rang, and TJ came flying into my room. My dad woke up to answer it, and all we heard was, "They're in bed... Fairhaven Police Station?? What??"

We had no clue if Doug got bagged or what was happening with Mud. My pops started yelling, asking what the fuck was going on. We told him we didn't know anything about anything. He took us to the police station.

When we got there, an officer was on the phone with Doug's mother, telling her to bring him in. She told the cop she didn't have cab money for that bullshit and if they wanted

The Great Solar Stance

Doug, they better come pick him up. Then she hung up on him. The phone was crazy loud, and TJ and I were cracking up.

The cops questioned us, said a few officers were injured in the crash, gave us our arraignment papers, and sent us home. My father didn't say a word the entire ride. He was pissed. He knew we got down on that shit.

The next day, TJ and I went to Mud's crib to check on him. He answered the door on crutches; arms wrapped in ace bandages. He told us that when he saw TJ and I hop over the guardrail onto the hill, he thought grass ran along the whole rail. Too late, he realized the section he jumped over only had Route 18 below it—a 40-foot drop.

He landed in the middle of the highway. Broke his ankle. Both shoulders popped out of the socket. When we heard him screaming "Five-Oh," he was calling for help so he wouldn't get hit by a car doing 60 mph while he lay there unable to move.

We exchanged stories and laughed. His mom was NOT happy. Jeannie gave us an earful that day.

Homegirl snitched, and I got hit with $2,000 restitution. My dad made me cash in some savings bonds he had for me since birth. I wanted to use those for clothes before college, but nope. I was trying to hit NYC shining.

Eventually, I got my acceptance letter from Five Towns College and scheduled a walkthrough. My brother-in-law Tony drove Mud and me to Long Island to check out the campus.

Sky King

Musicians were everywhere—in the cafeteria, the hallways, the common areas. The vibe had me hook, line, and sinker.

The Visit Coordinator told me there were no dorms, but the school had housing at the Plainview Hotel in the next town over. I was gassed—crazy anxious to start college. I cashed in my remaining bonds and bought mad gear. Clothes and sneakers galore.

In August 1993, my dad took me to the school to get my books, pay for the semester, and attend orientation. That's when I met Pete—he had some B-boy in him. He was cool. After orientation, all the students left. Classes didn't start for two weeks, so instead of going home, I stayed. The hotel had a meal plan, so my dad bought me a booklet of coupons for meals.

For a week, I just read Stephen King books and ate three meals a day. My man Lyle from Westlawn was at Columbia University and told me to hit him up when I got to NYC. We met at Penn Station and went to Columbia, then walked around 125th St. Within minutes, I saw Anthony Mason from the Knicks and Greg Nice and Smooth B chilling across the street. I was bugging—Lyle acted like it was just another day.

That night, we hit a jump-off at Columbia. Lyle introduced me to his boy Max, and we got into a debate about Mike Tyson vs. Evander Holyfield. I swore Tyson would win—Max broke it all down. I told him, "Man, you don't know what you're talking about."

The Great Solar Stance

Years later, I saw Max on TV giving boxing takes. It was Max Kellerman. I told Max Kellerman he didn't know boxing... AND the fight went exactly like he said it would. Shame on me. After the parties that night Lyle showed me which train to take back to Penn station. It's about 3 a.m. and I'm the only person on the platform waiting for the train. That shit was nutty. I was waiting for some crazy motherfucker to come down those stairs and start some shit. I had a blade in my hand ready to go if needed. I made it back to Long Island without incident. I spent the next week reading and eating three times a day. I'm a full-blown introvert so it was easy being alone.

All the students that were staying at the hotel started arriving the day before classes started. Everybody was meeting their roommates. I had just finished eating and when I got back to my spot, there was a skin head dude with combat boots unloading his gear. He said his name was Harley. Uh Oh!!! What gives?? How is this going to work? I saw Pete going next door and he got turntables. His roommate was sort of on the same level as mine so Pete and I brainstormed a plan to get them to switch with us. Pete moved his turntables into my room.

Pete was an emcee, DJ, and beatmaker. He was part of a crew called I.V.S. (International Vibe Squad). We got along well, so I felt comfortable around him. He told me I could get on his set whenever I wanted and didn't even have to ask. Then he sparked up some trees—dude always had weed.

Sky King

Classes started the next day, and I was ready to rock. I wore a green Nike hoodie, a yellow Eddie Bauer vest, and a pair of green and yellow Nike Air Max. As I walked through the cafeteria, some young female looked me up and down and said, "I like the Sprite in you." That told me everything I needed to know—this year was going to be dope. All the girls thought I was Puerto Rican. Everybody kept confusing my name, Vernon, with my ethnicity, Cape Verdean. When people asked my name, I'd say, "Vernon." Then they'd ask if I was Puerto Rican. When I told them I was Cape Verdean, 100% of the time, they'd respond with, "You're Cape Vernon?" It was nuts.

After dinner that night, I went back to my room, and when I walked in, Harley from next door was sitting Indian-style and barefoot on my bed. If there's one thing I hate, it's feet—I don't want anyone's bare feet anywhere near me. I told Harley, "We're not doing that around here. Get your feet off my shit." He got right up and sat on the floor at the foot of my bed.

Pete was lighting up, so there were a few people hanging out in our spot. Cooly and Davy, roommates from down the walkway, were official weed heads. Pete and I were always with them. Davy had so much trash and seeds in his car that a plant sprouted in the back seat. That shit was crazy. Those were the dudes who put me onto Seinfeld. They were faithful watchers. Honestly, I think all the students who lived in the hotel were drug abusers that watched Seinfeld.

The Great Solar Stance

Davy had pulled out a bottle of ketamine. I had never even heard of that shit before. Cooly knew exactly how to chef it up. He poured some on a mirror, put a lightbulb under it, and when it cooked up and dried, he scraped it with a razor and sprinkled it on his blunt. That was a weird high. We would get high and play Street Fighter all day.

Cooly was studying audio recording and had to record a song for an exam. He wanted Pete and me to write verses about Bob Ross' TV show, The Joy of Painting. That was THE illest song I ever made in my life. Pete could get busy on the rhymes. It was a good time, though—my first time being in an official music studio. Five Towns had a few of them. I was studying music business management, but my classes were boring as hell. I loved the common areas in between classes. One time, I walked up on a rhyme cipher. I rocked them with the off-the-top rhyme style we used to splash at Mud's crib. They weren't ready for that. Dudes were like, "Who the fuck are you?" I'm V-Nek from New B! I can't remember any of their names. There were rhyme sessions happening all over that school.

We got cool with this kid named Lenny. Lenny sold pounds for his father, so Pete and I went to his house so Pete could cop something. When we got there, Lenny showed us his beat-making room. He had an SP-1200. That was the first time I had ever seen one in person. I knew Pete Rock used it to make *Mecca & The Soul Brother*. We messed around with it for a while. Pete was familiar with the SP-1200, so I was telling

Sky King

him about the Ensoniq EPS, but he had never heard of it. I thought the EPS was better because it could do everything the SP1200 could and had piano keys. Plus, the EPS had way more sample time.

Pete sold me an ounce for cheap. I bagged it up and flipped it at school. The thought of getting kicked out for selling weed made me put that to a halt. I didn't want to have to explain that to my parents.

I went home for one of the holidays and brought Ricky back with me to stay for a week. This dude is the illest. He showed up with a Shaw's Supermarket plastic bag with a few pairs of boxers and socks in it, just counting on wearing my gear for the week. About ten minutes after we got settled, Ricky got up to use the bathroom. Cooly comes over and sits in the chair Ricky had been sitting in, with his back to the bathroom. Ricky came out, walked up behind Cooly, slapped him in the back of the head, and said, "Damn, nigga, you just gonna jump in my grave like that?" Cooly had no idea Ricky was there—he was shook.

The next wild thing was Ricky arguing with my cousin Cerrie on Pete's phone. At the end of their conversation, Ricky started slamming the receiver against the bottom half of the phone console. He must've banged that shit about five or six times until the hang-up button broke. Pete looked at me like, what is up with your man?

The grand finale of the Ricky trip was when Pete took us to some projects in Wyandanch, Long Island to grab some

The Great Solar Stance

trees. Ricky and I stayed in the car while Pete went inside. Ricky asked if I thought he could get out of the car, run up to the porch, and piss on it before they came out. I told him, "Nah, bro, don't do that."

He got right out of the whip and pissed on the porch anyway. Three seconds after he got back in the car, Pete and the dude came out. They could smell the urine. They looked down, saw the piss on the porch and the wall, then looked at us in the car before finishing their conversation. The dude went back in the house, and Pat got back in the car. This shit was crazy because the porch light was bright as hell. Anyone looking out their window would've seen him. That was an unforgettable week.

Ricky would just stay in my room, writing rhymes, while we were all in Cooly's room, smoking L after L. I gave him the coins I had saved up so he could buy a bus ticket back to New Bedford. He thought my baby blue and gray Air Max were going back to New B with him. But they weren't.

Pete asked me if I wanted to take a ride out to Riverhead to pick up his man Wise. I didn't have anything else to do, so I was like, "Word." Wise was one of the purest B-Boys I had ever met—his slang, his mannerisms, everything about him was the epitome of Hip-Hop culture. It was like someone had pulled him straight out of a graffiti black book. He was the character all the graff writers were drawing.

He tells Pete he needs to go to the Bronx to grab some Dust. We hit his plug's spot, he gets back in, and then says he

Sky King

needs to head down to Fordham Rd. and Webster Ave. We go into one of the stores, and I spotted Carla DaCosta and Mike B from New Bedford. Carla sees me and says, "Look at the schoolboy." What were the chances of running into people I knew from little-ass New Bedford in a random store in the Bronx? That was nuts.

Wise buys some gear, and then we head back to Long Island. They asked me if I've ever smoked Dust before. I say "no," and Wise smirks. "Buckle up... you're going for a ride, kid."

He rolls a blunt of straight Dust. No weed. Just straight illy. I swear I was counting every single dash on the highway from the Bronx back to my room. We pull up, Pete opens our door, and the moment I see his turntables, I start unhooking them to take them back to my room. But we were already in my room. I was fucking HIGH.

Pete drove Wise back to Riverhead and stayed the night at his family's home in East Quogue. Meanwhile, I was tripping all by myself.

The next day, I woke up all fucked up. Cooly calls me, tells me to come down to his room, says I need to puff a little something to get focused. I walk in, and he hands me a bong. He lights the bowl, and I start pulling without even looking. Instantly, I feel the cold intake of air and taste the mint. Motherfucker. I had just taken a big ass hit of Dust from a bong.

The Great Solar Stance

I had to go back to my room and lay down. My heart was racing a million miles per hour. I thought I was going to die. I kept thinking about how my mother would react to finding out I overdosed on Dust. Everything was spinning. That was a crazy trip—it felt like I didn't come down for hours. I was fucking scared. But I'm not scared enough to learn my lesson.

One time, Pete and his man Eugene came through with mushrooms. I was down to try it. We scooped up three girls from Brooklyn, and we all got shroomed out. Huh. That was a crazy night.

I started off with one girl in my bed. Woke up with two girls in my bed. We were eating those mushrooms like Cheez-Its. I still didn't learn my lesson.

I had used my last meal ticket for breakfast, so I went to the hotel office to get more coupons for dinner. I wasn't expecting to hear that I wasn't getting any more. To get more, I had to pay for another meal plan. Unbeknownst to me, the meal plan was designed for one free meal a day. I had been using three, sometimes four, a day. Oh shit.

I checked the Student Center for job listings and found one directly across the street from my room at JSE Distribution Center. I couldn't deal with that place— same old repetitive work all night. I quit after two weeks. And you know what I did? Yep… started selling weed again. Nothing major— just enough to eat every day. I hated calling my father for money.

Sky King

On my way to the lobby, I passed my next-door neighbor's room and couldn't believe my eyes. Sitting on his table was an Ensoniq EPS. The Hip Hop Gods had shined light upon me once again. Turns out his grandmother bought it for him, but he barely used it. He told me I could rock with it anytime he was around. The problem? He was never around. I even asked if I could borrow it, I was only next door! He wasn't having it. Damn. I wanted to show Pete that the EPS was better than the SP-1200, but I never got the chance.

Not making music was driving me crazy. None of the students at the hotel made beats. This shit was lame. I couldn't wait for the semester to end—I needed to be around my people.

The second semester was going to be different. Pete, Cooly, and Davy split the rent on a three-bedroom apartment not far from the hotel. My new roommate, Dante, was cool as hell. He was hardly ever in the room—dude was shacking up with some girl on the Island—so I basically had the space to myself. As an introvert, that worked out perfectly for me.

My room was now on the second floor in the back tier, where some wild parties went down. One night, this short white kid named Sam came through, chopping it up with Pete and me before one of the jump-offs started. He was telling us about his girl—how beautiful she was—and about all the times he'd been jumped, stabbed, and even shot at defending her honor. He said guys were always trying to pull her, and since he thought we were cool, he hoped we wouldn't be on that

The Great Solar Stance

type of time because she was coming to the party that night. Everyone in the room reassured him there wouldn't be any issues.

An hour or two later an exotic super model with an extremely voluptuous figure walked through the door with Sam. This girl looked like the most beautiful Asian, Italian and African mixture that nature could come up with. It was the craziest thing because Sam reminds me of the fat kid from the Superbad movie. A low budget Jonah Hill stunt double. It didn't make sense. When they walked in the energy of the party changed. It went from zero to a hundred quick. The intensity of the music even amped up. The wolves moved in—subtly, of course—but the liquor had already been flowing. Every move she made, she had a crowd of guys around her. No one was outright disrespectful, but I remember looking at Sam, dude had his head in his hands, just shaking it.

Later that night, Sam started talking to Pete about his coke connects in the Bronx. Pete was trying to cop, so we made a trip out there the next day. I had nothing else going on, so I tagged along. That trip turned out to be the wildest shit I've ever been involved in.

We pulled up to this apartment building that looked completely abandoned—five or six stories high, no blinds or curtains, maybe the windows were painted black. As we walked up to the door, I got a bad feeling. Sam banged on the door, and a pair of eyes peered through a metal slider. He stated who he was and what we were there for. After some yelling from the other side, the door cracked open. A man stood there holding an Uzi.

He rushed us inside, frisked us, and shoved us up the stairs. As we climbed to the top floor, we passed armed sentries on every landing, each one gripping a machine gun. When we finally got to the top, we were ushered into what used to be an apartment—but most of the walls had been torn down, making it an open floor concept plan. Smack in the middle of the space was a desk with a triple beam scale. Armed guards stood all around.

A dark-skinned man with broken English asked Sam what we wanted. Sam told him: two ounces. The man snapped his fingers, and another guy stepped out from behind a wall with the goods. He put them on the scale, confirmed the weight, and Pete handed over the money. Just like that, we were ushered back out. Before we left, they frisked us again. I don't know what for, but those motherfuckers were making sure they weren't getting robbed. Anyone who tried would have had zero chance of making it out alive. I walked into that mess with two white boys. I was certain I was going to die that night.

Back at school, my man Nick came through to light me up and brought a stack of kung fu flicks with him. He knew how I got down, so he even brought his VCR so I could dub them with mine. He had all the classics. When I wasn't in class, I'd just sit in my room, get high, and watch kung fu movies all day.

The Great Solar Stance

In April of '94, I planned a weekend trip home. Something told me I wouldn't be coming back, so I packed up all my clothes and kicks in two big duffle bags.

At Huntington Station, waiting for the train to Penn, the wolves spotted me. My gear was on point—fresh all black Timberlands, looking right. A group of young boys was with an OG, and the old cat looked me up and down before saying, "Those are mine."

I was sitting in the corner, minding my business but keeping my eye on them. Did this dude just claim my boots? Ah, shit. They were about eight deep—this could get ugly.

When my train arrived, all eyes were on me. But they hadn't anticipated the rush of people getting off. I grabbed my bags and disappeared into the crowd, slipping onto the train. As we pulled off, I watched them scanning the platform, looking for me. I threw them the finger. Fuck those little dirty-looking niggers. And that's niggers with a hard ER.

When I got back to New Bedford, I felt comfortable. It was my first time home since January. Mud had moved to Verdean Gardens across from the Bay Village projects. I was supposed to catch the bus back to New York, but as I sat in his room, I realized something—I didn't want to go back.

I wasn't feeling creative out there. I hadn't made any music the whole time I was in New York. But here, at Mud's, we were always working on something new. I made up my mind and called my father. I knew he was going to be hot. My mother started riffing about the money he had paid for two

Sky King

semesters. Yeah, I had fucked up. But I wasn't happy there. The vibe wasn't right.

A few weeks later, I went back to grab my stereo and the rest of my stuff. I've never regretted not finishing school. It just wasn't for me.

Chapter Fifteen
These Tu Bum Emcees

Shortly after I returned to New Bedford, some group—I can't remember who—announced they were putting on a show. At that time, Ricky, Mud, Spank, and I were always together. These guys formed my musical foundation. Spank and I went down to the Armory to sign up for the show. When the girl asked for our group's name, I was at a loss because we didn't officially have one yet. I spontaneously said, "The Four Deadly Venoms". We watched Five Deadly Venoms almost every day. It seemed fitting. Ultimately, the show never happened, and we never used that name again.

While hanging out at Mud's place, we were messing around, freestyling, when Ricky suddenly dropped a verse about jerking off over Run DMC's *Sucker MC's* beat. It was hilariously unexpected—so much so that I felt compelled to write my own verse about jerking off. It was a humorous type of joint. We recorded the track at Mud's, and dudes were playing that shit in their whips. Driving around banging a song about masturbating. Shit was crazy. After that, we started calling ourselves "These Tu Bum Emcees."

Mud's crib was the center of our universe, and we spent most of our time in the South End. None of us were involved in the West End vs. South End beef, so we maintained good relationships with many of our South End high school friends. Monte's Park was known for getting money. Mud and Ricky started making money, too. Spank and I, however, still spent considerable time uptown in the West End. He would pick me up around ten o'clock every morning, and we'd head to the bodega on Chancery and Kempton, hustling up some change to buy a dime bag. We'd stand outside the bodega for hours. Scott Buddah and his crew were usually on Chancery, near Nort's parking lot, while everyone else congregated at the "U" inside United Front. If you rocked with the West End, you'd be around either Westlawn, the Front, or often both.

At the time, Mike Nice was known as the consignment king, helping everyone get started. I asked him to front me an ounce of bud, and he agreed. Eventually, I saved enough from consignments to buy my own quarter pound. Around this period, I took custody of Le'Rynn from her grandmother, and she came to live with me. She would often be with me at Monte's while I made my plays. Looking back, I was young and reckless. Though I briefly had a job at Pizza Hut, selling weed was simply easier.

My friend Cory Garcia was organizing a show at Boston College and invited us to open for Nice & Smooth. Of course,

The Great Solar Stance

we were down. Some guys from Monte's offered to rent a car to drive us up. Saadiq insisted he'd squeeze in the rental somehow. We crammed an unbelievable number of guys into that van, along with guns, drugs, and even a few people with warrants. When we arrived, Cory had us hang out in the hockey team's locker room until showtime. Ill & Al Scratch and Ed O.G. were also performing that night.

We wanted to smoke but had no blunts. Al Scratch walked by with a Philly blunt tucked in his backward tennis visor. I asked if he had extras, but he said he didn't and added he didn't smoke weed. Some guys started clowning him, but he just walked away.

I looked out onto the ice and spotted someone walking with a familiar strut. As he got closer, we realized, "Oh shit, is that Kyle?" Indeed, it was Kyle Watkins and a group from the Front, there to support us—and he had blunts. The atmosphere grew tense. We had come with about six South End guys, now in a bathroom smoking with about twelve West End guys, some were known to be hostile. Luckily, everything stayed peaceful, but at any given moment it could have gone sideways.

Our performance went well, but when we did the jerking-off joint, it seemed the crowd wasn't quite ready for it. Thinking about it now, performing that song must have sounded fucking nuts. Afterward, Cory told us he'd secured a hotel room. Some groupies, mistaking us for a signed act, wanted to party. We lit up heavy in the hotel room, but even

Sky King

blasting the hot shower couldn't mask the smoke. Soon, Boston police knocked at the door. They searched the room but couldn't find any weed. Still, hotel management kicked us out. As we drove away, I worried about getting pulled over since we had a gun in the car with nowhere to hide it. Thankfully, the cops didn't bother us, and we had an uneventful ride home.

Chapter Sixteen
The Ensoniq EPS

1994 was a dope year for Hip Hop. Nas dropped *Illmatic*, and Gang Starr released *Hard To Earn*. Spank and I would hit Words and Music on release day for all the fly albums. I copped Biggie's *Ready to Die*, but I wasn't really a fan. We went back to Spank's crib to peep it, and maybe one song resonated with me. Those beats just didn't speak to me, so I gave my tape to Spank. I was feeling Method Man's *Tical* and Gravediggaz's *6 Feet Deep*. But one of my favorite albums that year was Jeru the Damaja's *The Sun Rises In The East*. DJ Premier put in massive work throughout '94.

My biggest inspiration that year wasn't musical, though. Sharnae told me she was pregnant, and I immediately knew it was going to be a boy. I was alright with the situation because Sharnae had always held me down, whether it was food, sneakers, or weed. She always came through for me. On July 10, 1995, Shazan Shallah Gilmette was born. I named him after one of my favorite cartoon characters from *Hanna-Barbera's World of Super Adventures*. Sharnae lived with her mother in

Sky King

United Front, and just before giving birth, her mom planned to move out and pass the apartment to Sharnae. Le'Rynn and I moved into Sharnae's spot the same day Shazan came home from the hospital.

1995 was filled with blessings. Not only did I become a father for the second time, but my man Alan from the Townhouses informed me his cousin had an Ensoniq EPS he could lend me until he needed it back. WHAT?! LET'S GET IT! We called Alan "Big A" sometimes "Big A from the Shelter," partly because ODB ended a song with that line and partly because Big A always had food in the fridge. Big A's crib soon became known as "the Shelter." And come to find out, Manny Carter is Big A's uncle. I shit you not. It's crazy how everything connects. He delivered on his promise and dropped the EPS off at my mother's house. I got straight to work.

'95 also brought me Knowledge of Self. Mud's cousin BJ returned from school in Atlanta as Born Justice and started dropping jewels on us daily. Born introduced us to the Supreme Mathematics, Supreme Alphabet, and the 120 degrees of knowledge, wisdom, and understanding. My love for reading had kicked into high gear—I spent hours studying lessons and buying every book I could get my hands on. Spank and I even stole a couple of books. That's when I transformed into Viktory God Allah, inspired by my initials in the Supreme Alphabet. Most folks just called me God V.

1995 kept delivering gifts. Within four months, Hip Hop received *Only Built for Cuban Linx* and *Liquid Swords*. These

The Great Solar Stance

albums weren't just teaching me about myself; they showed me how to construct songs. I didn't want to make tracks with repetitive, looping beats. I always envisioned my songs having action. Now, with the EPS, I can sit down and carefully plan my approach. The EPS didn't have a pre-installed sound library—you had to load, or sample sounds yourself. I borrowed keyboards from anyone that had one just so I could sample the sounds to build my own library. I didn't have a turntable yet, so I sampled mostly from CDs.

I was trying to define my style and learn to create the music I envisioned. About a year later, the day I dreaded finally arrived, Big A's cousin needed the keyboard back. Damn! That hurt. Still, it was better to have loved and lost than never to have loved at all. I still had my disks loaded with beats and sounds. Mike Nice told me he found an EPS online for $700. At the time, I was selling weed and working at Titleist, so the $700 sounded good. Mike went to pick it up, but the seller got funky at the last minute, upping the price to $750. Mike covered the extra $50, and I became the proud owner of an Ensoniq EPS 16 Plus—the newer model with more sampling time.

Mike had started a DJ company with Mud as the DJ, regularly hosting parties. Mike had purchased serious equipment: Technics turntables, amps, speakers—the entire setup. He offered to keep my EPS at his place, so I had easy access to everything, and we could vibe out and smoke, something I couldn't do at my mother's house. Mike lived right

Sky King

across the street from me, making the arrangement perfect. And it got even sweeter.

I don't recall all the specifics, but Mike had an agreement with his uncle about buying his uncle's house. Mike began renovations and planned to build a music studio in the basement. His friend Bob, a skilled carpenter, agreed to soundproof the studio and build a vocal booth. They followed through completely—Mike built me a studio. We didn't have recording equipment yet, but the structure was complete. Located on Sycamore Street, just two blocks from my mother, everything was falling into place. I planned to stack money to invest in the equipment we needed.

Weed sales were booming; my dime bags were the biggest around, known as "God V bags." For $10, you could split the bag into three, smoke one, and still make $20.

Chapter Seventeen
Scotty Watt

Mike Barboza was promoting a Jay-Z show at Stargazers and asked us to open for him. This was right after *Ain't No Nigga* came out, so we were down. Mike B hooked us up with about ten bottles of liquor as payment—shit was wild. Backstage, we were getting completely wasted. Scotty Watt came back, hyping me up: "Yo V, rip that shit!" Then he immediately threw up on the floor right by the gate.

Jungo was hanging backstage with us when security approached and told him he had to leave. Jungo insisted he was with us, but the bouncers weren't hearing it. He refused to go, and things started getting tense. The bouncers were huge—one was Jeff McCoy, big, strong, athletic, and could fight. The other was a massive white guy. I was drunk as hell and had butterflies in my stomach, knowing I was about to perform. I ended up throwing up right at the bottom of the backstage stairs.

Just as I started puking, security grabbed Jungo and tried to toss him out. Jungo started manhandling both bouncers, tossing these big dudes around with ease. But his advantage didn't last long—he slipped in my vomit and hit the floor. Jeff immediately began pounding Jungo in the ribs. (The crazy thing is, when I saw Jungo the next day at United Front playing basketball, he didn't even know big Jeff had crashed out on his ribs. He ate all that shit.) Eventually, security dragged him out of the backstage area.

I was so drunk that I forgot my rhymes and had to freestyle the entire set. I don't think anyone noticed. Guys in the crowd were throwing bags of weed up on stage. Later, during Jay-Z's performance, it looked like a fight broke out. Someone mentioned that someone got stabbed. On our way out, Barry told me Scotty had been stabbed but he would be okay. Sharnae's cousin, Shante, had been babysitting for us that night. When we got home, she told us Scotty Watt had died.

I immediately called Quasi's house, and the way Janice answered confirmed the worst. Scotty Watt—one of the realest dudes I'd ever known—was gone. The next day, I grabbed a can of spray paint and wrote, "There will never be another Scotty Watt," on the sidewalk on Chancery Street in front of Quasi's crib. His death impacted a lot of people. Everybody loved Scotty. May the Universe be pleased with him.

Chapter Eighteen
The Raid

March 21, 1997. It was a typical Friday. I woke up, got dressed, and started selling weed like any other day. Sharnae left with her mother, and I stayed home with Shazan. Le'Rynn was with her grandmother. I rolled a blunt and put on The Mystery of Chessboxing. There were always kung fu flicks playing in the crib; movies and music were constant. My brother Boo came over to smoke, and I cuffed him an ounce since I'd just picked up a pound the night before.

We were watching the flick when suddenly we heard a loud bang. If you know anything about United Front, you're familiar with some hallway doors. If you needed a place to smoke, you could open certain hallway doors and sit on the bottom steps. Initially, I thought someone was smoking in the hall. Then another bang, followed by another. Now I'm thinking its kids playing around, so I yell, "You little niggas better get out of my hallway!" There was another bang, this one shaking my back door. When I saw the door move, I thought it might be my brother Kippy coming for my brother

Sky King

Boo—they had serious beef at the time. But I knew he wouldn't act wild where his niece and nephew lived.

While calculating all this, both doors burst open, and cops rushed in and put their guns to my head. "Where's the coke? Where's the coke?" I'm thinking, "Who the fuck got coke?" They showed me the warrant and began flipping furniture. I told them I didn't have cocaine. Since my weed wasn't hidden, I offered to get it to avoid them wrecking the apartment. Sharnae was a neat freak and would flip out seeing the mess. I had the pound in a Nike shoebox in my closet, which they'd easily find, so I handed it over. They calmed down after that, minimizing the damage while continuing to search.

The captain asked me to call someone to pick up Shazan, so I called Mike's wife, who arrived quickly. The cops were annoyed they'd only found a pound of weed. One asked about my brother, and they decided to let him go without checking his backpack—so he walked away with the ounce I'd given him.

I was taken downtown, with a forty-dollar bail. They took my weed and money, $1,400 from my bureau and $750 from my pocket. After about half an hour in a filthy cell, Sharnae bailed me out. The cell was nasty—feces smeared on the blanket. On the way home, Sharnae let me have it.

Luckily, we argued a few days earlier. Fed up with me running the streets, she'd thrown my triple beam scale at me, breaking it against the wall. I'd tossed it out—thankfully,

The Great Solar Stance

because having it during the raid would've meant another charge.

After cleaning up, I noticed my scrambler and rhyme book were missing. Scramblers were old school—you could watch pay-per-view events for free. Roy Jones was fighting Montell Griffin that Friday night, and I couldn't watch. I was steaming, more upset about missing the fight than the raid itself. (Ironically, a few years later, one of those same cops got arrested during a sweep at the police station for using illegal cable scramblers.) But why did they take my rhyme book?

I called my father, explained what happened, and endured a fifteen-minute verbal lashing. He was deeply disappointed. He knew many cops, so I asked him to retrieve my rhyme book. He came through, but when he returned it, he was tipsy and lectured me again.

Another issue was potential eviction—United Front policy dictated eviction after raids. Sharnae and I proactively planned to move out. On Monday, we went to the office to inform them. When the manager asked why, we said we needed a three-bedroom so Le'Rynn and Shazan wouldn't share a room. Surprisingly, she immediately offered us a three-bedroom apartment. Sharnae and I were stunned but ecstatic. We moved from our third-floor Chancery Street apartment to a two story, three-bedroom on Morgan Street. It felt like a blessing.

Around this time, Spank and Saadiq took over Poopie's apartment on Court Street—our new ground zero. The studio

Sky King

Mike was building fell through due to issues between him and his uncle. We lost the studio, and Mike shut down his DJing operation. Then, surprisingly, Mike gave me his brand-new Technic 1200 turntables, a Tascam 16-track mixing board, and a computer with Cakewalk recording software. We couldn't get the software to work properly, so he kept it, but I kept the turntables and mixing board.

Chapter Nineteen
Revolutionary Minds

Now that I have a bigger apartment, I finally have more room. With the extra space, I can keep my EPS close and get busy whenever inspiration hits. My setup includes two turntables, a Tascam 16-track mixing board, an Ensoniq EPS, and a Pioneer stereo receiver with speakers. It's time to get busy.

I created a beat using the piano melody from the theme song of *Love Story*. Saadiq and I each wrote verses, shaping the song into something serious. We recorded it using Mud's four-track. Mud found a dope scratch from Richard Pryor's album, *That Nigger's Crazy*, specifically a bit where Richard impersonates a preacher beginning a conversation with God, saying, "Ya know, God..." Mud absolutely nailed those scratches for the hook. We named the track *Mind War*, and it could arguably be considered the first official Seven Headed Angel song. When we played it on WSMU 91.1, people loved it. This might be the beginning of my scientific rhyme style.

Sky King

Watch the sky's rotations
Count twelve constellations
I speak to my solar
To intrigue him with calculations
Conversations made to maintain
The battle stations
Expect the unexpected
And take drastic preparations
Explanations of the fabulous places
My mind has been to
Fascination of the worlds
That both rhyme and mind have been through
As my travels throughout this world will still continue,
It's in you Godly power is within you
Back since the creation of it all
Mankind prays that my lyrication
Will never ever fall
Situations that I recall
Are the explanations of it all
Origination of the wizardry
Mental complication is a downfall
Plus, decreases capability
Your mental stamina facility
Must maintain its composure and agility
This utility, the microphone Is my tool
To maintain my status
On this land that I rule

The Great Solar Stance

Next up was a Ricky solo track titled "*The Combat Show.*" By this point, Ricky had transformed into Ricky Combat—just one of his many aliases. That recording session was challenging. It was the scorching summer of '97, and we were working in my bedroom with no fan, no AC, just pure determination. Mud skillfully scratched the GZA line, "Who flips the mic so well?" We took this track directly to the radio, further boosting our reputation.

Our notoriety was growing again, and we felt it was crucial to let everyone know exactly where we stood. Whenever I appeared on the radio, I spoke very arrogantly, it was simply an expression of how deeply my *solar stance* ran. That B-Boy attitude was ingrained in me.

Around this time, my friend Lenny Ramos approached me about contributing some tracks for a compilation album he was putting together with his partner Ace. The album, titled "Revolutionary Minds," would feature artists from New Bedford and Providence. I submitted both *Mind War* and *The Combat Show*. Len and Ace liked the tracks and decided that all artists would record at Midi Plus Studio in Fall River, owned and engineered by Rob Leonardo. Rob was incredibly knowledgeable, and I learned a great deal about professional recording from him.

Another New Bedford group, Busted Fro—consisting of Tem Blessed, Isotope, and DJ Wall Gee—also joined the compilation. I knew Tem from our time at Carney Academy;

Sky King

he lived in United Front when he was younger. I didn't know Isotope or Wall Gee prior to working on this album. Something about Isotope stood out to me. For one, his voice was powerful, and for two, I felt he worshipped lyrics the way I did. Rhode Island groups Roolette and Flow also participated, along with music contributions from Len and Ace themselves.

The sessions at Midi Plus were my first experiences in a professional studio environment, guided by a highly skilled engineer. Rob showed me how to optimize my EPS workflow, emphasizing efficiency and time management. After completing the album, my entire approach to recording music had shifted. I realized the four-track could no longer produce final master recordings, though it remained useful for song blueprints, a more professional method was essential.

Chapter Twenty
Digital

I was introduced to Spoonie June by Ricky around '93 or so. Ricky knew him from the Brickenwood projects and even bought an Audi from him. Spoonie had formed a Latino-based rap group called Lethal Package. He was cool as shit and always showed me love. One day I saw him downtown, and he gave me his number, telling me to call so we could set up a time for me to check out his studio. Spoonie lived in the School Street apartments down in the south end and had his studio set up right in his crib.

When I came through, Spoonie showed me how his studio worked and played some of Lethal Package's music. The quality was impressive, both sonically and substantively. They were recording on a Fostex DMT-8, a digital eight-track recorder. It operated on the same principle as Mud's four-track, but without the need for cassettes—and it had twice the number of tracks. I knew right away I had to get one.

I reached out to my father, asking if he could help me out by buying a Fostex DMT-8. He went to Rick's Music in

Sky King

Swansea and got me the eight-track recorder along with the multi-track expansion unit for my EPS. Rob Leonardo had tipped me off about this expansion unit, which allowed each sample track in the EPS to have separate outputs. Since I had a 16-track board, having an eight track recorder combined with eight instrument tracks was perfect. My studio setup was finally coming together.

Around this time, Spoonie was looking to upgrade his studio desk, so he asked if I was interested in buying his old one, along with his DAT recorder. I needed something to record master versions of my tracks, so I agreed. Shortly after buying the DAT machine, my father asked if I wanted a CD recorder because someone down at the club was selling one. I enthusiastically agreed, but when he brought it home, I realized it wasn't a CD recorder—it was a Sony Minidisc recorder. Minidiscs were more durable than CDs, resistant to scratching, and perfect for mastering my recordings.

Chapter Twenty-One
Seven Headed Angel

Spank is a graffiti writer. And when it comes to tagging, he has exquisite calligraphy. Whenever he's around pen and paper, he's bound to start tagging. I went to Spank and Saadiq's crib on Court Street to smoke, and as I sat down, I noticed one of his tagged papers. The most prominent tag was **Seven Headed Dragon**. In '95, '96, and '97, Spank and I were on a book kick, consuming vast amounts of information and having daily discussions on esoteric topics. Seeing the Seven Headed Dragon tag resonated deeply with me—I imagined the dragon as evil and envisioned its opposite: an angel. Thus, the concept of **Seven Headed Angel** was born.

I suggested Spank tag Seven Headed Angel, and it looked beautiful. I proposed starting a crew named Seven Headed Angel, and Spank, who was hard to impress, agreed immediately confirming it was indeed a solid idea. I figured the squad would include myself, Spank, Mud, Ricky, Saadiq, and Sabu. Although we didn't have seven members, the Angel symbolized one unified entity. I reached out to everyone individually, and they unanimously agreed. We officially became the Seven Headed Angel Crew.

A few of us were dealing with the teachings of The Nation of Gods and Earths at the time. Ricky Combat transformed into Ricky Culture, with his surname starting with "C," he had a boatload of ways to apply the science to his name. My friend Lamont Ferg mentioned knowing a talented girl who could draw and offered to ask her for logo ideas. We dove right in. Booking studio time at Midi Plus at $35 an hour, we recorded our first song, *Battle in the Sky*, with Bu and myself. Ricky, Saadiq, and I each laid verses on *48 Bars of Fire*, and Ricky and I created *Counter React Maneuver*. Bu had a standout solo joint titled *Edukayshun*. Rob provided us with a rough CD mix, though the master recordings were stored on two-inch reels, standard analog technology at the time.

We were in the Townhouses playing the CD for some people when Jungo asked if he could run over to his mom's crib to burn a copy of the joints. He said he would make me another CD as well. I didn't have a CD burner, so I was with it. He bounced with the CD and that was the last time I saw that shit. It was just our luck that the reel ended up getting ruined along with a lot of my old records. We never went back to Midi Plus. As we were putting the pieces back together, I was approached by a young kid who introduced himself as Ralz. He told me that he was Jungo's younger brother. You know I asked him about that CD, but he didn't know anything about it. He said that he rhymed and needed some beats. His

The Great Solar Stance

DJ was my man Dana who was going by the name Boy Brown. Ralz spit some rhymes for me, and I thought he got busy, so I told him to come by the crib. They started coming through and we put some joints together. Nothing was finalized but we were working.

I was trying to get the SHA back into the lab, so I put together a song called *Seventh Sign*. The number seven played a big role in our approach. "G" is the seventh letter. We applied that to all kinds of ideas. Saadiq and Bu had verses on *Seventh Sign*. I did the hook. At the last minute I asked Ralz to be on the joint. He added new energy to the song. His style fit right in with us. 1998 also brought me my third blessing. Saejzan Shallahr Gilmette arrived on September 9th.

Dwayne Branco, aka DJ RareForm, was close with Mud and Spank. RareForm entered a DJ battle in New Jersey hosted by DJ Chuck Chillout as part of a music seminar and showcase. Brian Monteiro, owner of Sound City—a record store next to King Cuts, where Spank was a barber—offered to bring us to Jersey to audition for the music showcase. We planned on rocking *Seventh Sign*. Everyone except Bu Ruk made the trip.

Packed into Brian's Ford Expedition, we arrived in Newark to a crowded scene of auditioning rappers. Recognizing my anxiety, Saadiq had to pull me to the side and set me straight. He reminded me of why we were there and that it was easy work. When it was our turn to rock we had to perform over the actual song with the lyrics. The tape with the instrumental had popped on the way to New Jersey. Now I had to say Bu's verse because he was on the song. I thought rhyming over the vocals would be catastrophic, but we made it into the final show. Out of over a hundred acts we were one of the ten that made it. We had all kinds of jokes about Bu for not rolling when Ralz showed up and he wasn't even in the crew. On the ride home we voted to put Ralz in the squad. He became an official member of the Seven Headed Angel.

Brian got us hotel rooms for the night of the show. We rolled up to Newark in two Expeditions this time. I can't remember how much time we were allotted but we put together a fly routine. The Seven was ready to rock. While we were hanging out in one of the rooms the night before the show Brian said he wanted to see if we were official. He wanted to hear some off the top of the head rhymes. We went in with no hesitation. Ralz was especially gifted with the ability to go off the top for extended lengths of time. Somebody had put on the instrumental to The Beatnuts' *Watch Out Now*.

RareForm won the DJ battle. The prize was one thousand dollars. Chuck Chillout announced Dwayne as the winner then pulled some money out of his pocket. He counted it, realized that he didn't have enough money, then he asked the other judges to put in whatever money they had. RareForm was about to start some shit. Things were looking really sketchy. They came up with enough money so that calmed D down. When Chuck gave him the money, D told him that he only won because Mud didn't enter. Chuck said, "Show us what you got Mud". Mud got on the stage and did a quick one-minute display. Body rocked the whole shit. He blew Chuck's face off. Chuck asked Mud why he didn't enter the battle, and Mud just shrugged his shoulders as if to say, "I don't know".

It was time for the performances. We had a good solid showing. I felt good about it. The Hip Hop Gods didn't smile upon us that day. We came in second place. It might have been a good thing. Who knows? That management deal might have been fraudulent. The entire vibe was kind of suspect. It felt like a money grab because all the auditioning acts had to pay a fee. I wasn't discouraged at all. It was a good experience.

When we got back Brian said we should put out a CD and he would sell it exclusively in Sound City. He said he would have all the CD's pressed and have the covers printed. We wouldn't be charged for anything, and we could keep all the money from the sales. This was an opportunity we couldn't pass up.

We started to work on a Seven Headed Angel E.P. Lamont comes back with some preliminary sketches of a logo by Jacqueline Lesik. There were about four different ideas on the paper. One stood out amongst the others. I showed it to Brian, and he said he would give it to Eden to polish it up. Eden Soares had created the Sound City logo and painted the logo on the inside of the record shop. He took Jacqueline's idea and multiplied it by seven thousand. The logo came out dope. Everybody was happy with the final product. We were going to work on the music. Eden was going to create the CD cover.

Chapter Twenty-Two
The E.P

The first song we created was called *Wild Kingdom*. I made the beat, and Ralz instantly had a verse ready. Saadiq, Jungo, and Bu Ruk also joined the track. The second joint was *Revolution*, featuring Saadiq and Bu. These two songs were placed first and second, respectively, on the track list. While I don't recall the exact order of recording for the rest, creating Wild Kingdom and Revolution assured me this project would be incredible.

I recorded a solo track called *Viktorious Serahnade*. I just went in on a beat that inspired me to write. Ralz and Saadiq collaborated on *Angel Dust*, showcasing their big brother-little brother dynamic perfectly. Saadiq, Ralz, and I created *The Great Solar Stance*. When I crafted this beat, it radiated power; every time I played it, I envisioned myself in the B-Boy stance. Just waiting to explode on somebody. It was only right that we turned this beat into a song and named it The Great Solar Stance.

The Great Solar Stance

The term Great Solar Stance comes from a Jet Li movie, Kung Fu Cult Master. A banished monk with a broken back chained himself to a huge Indiana Jones type boulder to keep his spine intact. This monk was a master of the Great Sun Style. The English overdub version called it the Great Solar Stance. I immediately adopted this phrase after watching the film. It became the substitution for B-Boy stance. I had to get my shit off on this joint.

The Great Solar Stance

The solar mind,
the lunar gave birth—it's so refined
Quiet time, study the Earth—
it's so divine
Seven swords
obliterate yours with seven sweeps
Star travel exit the planet
with seven leaps
and visit nine spheres
they'll all be reached in nine years
With power amp megaphone mics,
we're pioneers.
Your time's here, cut you in half
with giant shears.
It's severe,
it rains like thousands of flying spears

Sky King

across the air, burn up the sky,
so be aware.
Holy warfare angel
that's rated beyond compare.
Super debonaire rhymer
invaded the Devil's lair. (The devil's lair, Seven Headed Angel)
The performance was so magnificent the world chants, "God V you're the greatest," and they all start to dance.
GREAT SOLAR STANCE.

I came up with an idea for a new joint called *This is God*. As soon as I put the beat together, I knew I wanted to go off the top of the head. I want to be perfectly clear. I DID NOT complete the verses for this song in one take. I did a few bars until I messed up. Then I punched in until I messed up again. I kept repeating this process until I finished both verses. The first verse is based on "This is God". The second verse is based on the number Seven. Ralz and I would go on to make a few more off the head joints on future albums. While I was recording *This is God*, I knew it would be special. I was enthusiastic about the outcome.

This is God

This is God the ruler
this is God the maker
this is God the creator
the giver and the taker

The Great Solar Stance

this is God you laughed at
this is God the man
this is God with the math that
most can't understand
this is God the master
of the Great Solar Stance
this is God that touched you
with the great golden lance
this is God your highness
this is God of all
this is God that formed your beautiful Earth
into a ball
this is God you called
this is God that came
this is God that manifests
every word inside his name
this is God that's so Viktorious
God is great
this is God with the madness
only Allah will demonstrate
this is God the flyest
climb the highest wall
this is God with the flyest rhyme
I never fall
this is God the meaning
this is God the word
this is God the animal

Sky King

this is God the bird
this is God the creature
this is God the teacher
this is God whose mightiest words
come through your speaker
this is God to reach you
this is God to teach you
this is God you pray to at night
and who you speak to
this is God of angels
this is God of wings
this is God of science
this is God of kings
this is God who allowed man
to walk the land
this is God to formulate rhymes
into a plan
this is God the champion
the winner of things
this is God to melt down your gold
and make seven rings
this is God the planet
it's God, you can't stand it
this is God that blew up the surface
it's too gigantic
this is God the holy
you say God sole control me

The Great Solar Stance

this is God that knows that he's God
because God told me....

Verse Two

Seven Gods came from out the sky
on Seven clouds
Seven Gods that rocked Seven mics
for Seven crowds
Seven ships to Pluto
make Seven trips to Jupiter
spread the Seven techniques
Seven miles from Lucifer
subtract the Seven ounces of brain
made him stupider
Seven Headed man
with Seven fingers on his hand
Seven is the science
Seven is he calling
Seven is the savior
you call him when you've fallen
Seven Headed God
it's the Seven Headed lord
Seven Headed Angel
production across the board
Seven Headed God stepped through
with Seven horns

Sky King

you met the Seven hurricane Gods
with Seven storms
Seven forms of punishment
made the Seventh song
Seven bucks to purchase the rhyme
you sing along
wrote a Seven on the wall
a Seven on the table
a solid gold Seven Headed charm
is on your cable
Seven is the alliance
Seven is the number
Seven is the science
that woke you out of your slumber
Seven is the wonder
Seven is wonderous
Seven is the thunder
Seven is thunderous
Seven is the God
that will put you on your ass
Seven is the owner
that will leave the Earth last
Seven is the reason
Seven is the season
Seven Headed mutilates devils
for their treason
Seven is the black man

The Great Solar Stance

Seven is the father
Seven is the light skin
creole God from Brava
Seven is the number
of oceans in the water
Seven is the sunshine
Seven is the daughter
Seven is the mother
Seven is the brother
Seven is the knowledge equality
you'll discover
Seven is the freedom justice equality
Seven Headed God Seven Headed policy....

The last song we recorded for the E.P was *Undah the Sun*. This was a Ralz solo joint. It was a standout on the project. Ralz came through with an apocalyptic crash of our civilization type concept. He always had a vision for his music and would get upset if it didn't coincide with the final product. It always worked out in the end.

We were all satisfied with the seven songs, so it was time to hand it over to Brian for duplication. The first question he asked after listening to it was "Why isn't Ricky on it?". We knew everybody was going to ask that same question. The answer was Ricky lived the fast life. At that moment, he didn't have the time to slow down to make music. He was still 100% on board and represented the project to the fullest degree. He was involved with all the promotion and advertising. Ricky and Ralz were the street team. I don't think anybody promoted the Seven Headed Angel crew more than Ricky, Ralz, Glizzo and Jungo. We had some stickers made and we put them up everywhere.

The final product was ready, and I couldn't have been more amped. There was no title. We just called it the Seven Headed Angel E.P. We released the CD on July 16th, 1999. It was only right to drop it on the sixteenth day of the seventh month. 1+6=7 and there are sixteen letters in SEVEN HEADED ANGEL.

When the CD dropped it felt like we instantly became ghetto celebrities. I would hear cars playing it as they drove by me, and I would think about the occupants of the car not even knowing that the dude they just passed was the producer of the music they were bumping.

Ben Gilbarg started a public access television show called Put Out the Word. He would highlight all aspects of the Hip Hop culture in our area. Put Out the Word was instrumental in widening our visibility. The show was under the umbrella of Ben's organization, 3rd Eye Unlimited. The feedback from the people was super positive. It wasn't just people that we knew gassing up their local crew. I had been in the King Kuts and overheard two kids speaking on the EP and not even knowing that God V was right there sitting in Spank's chair.

Ebony, Walt and I had gone to a party down south end. The DJ was playing Cape Verdean music, and all the creole girls were dancing. Eb said "V, go give the DJ a CD and tell him to play it". I wasn't with it because it felt like a creole jump off. Eb sucked his teeth, grabbed my CD and walked over to the DJ. Ten seconds later *Wild Kingdom* started playing and all the girls went crazy and started jamming to that shit. I was surprised. I did not think it was going to go down like that.

Ralz and Ricky went on a project tour. I don't mean "project" as in the CD. I mean they went through all the housing projects selling CDs. From South First all the way to Satellite Village. I'm a poor promotor. I don't have the stomach for it. I just want to make the music. These dudes were everywhere with it.

Kyle Watkins took the squad down to Florida to promote the music. I didn't roll with them. There was no way I could be in a vehicle for that amount of time. I don't like spending extended periods of time with other human beings. Saadiq, Ralz, Ricky and Jungo went. My understanding is that they ran into Krumb Snatcha from the Gang Starr Foundation and gave him a CD. I believe Jungo had done some time with him upstate. Sound City's phone number was on the CD. After they had returned from Miami Brian received a phone call from Krumb Snatcha and he was looking for information about the Seven. We set up a meeting and Krumb came to New Bedford.

As soon as he got out the car at Sound City he asked, "Who is God V"? We chopped it up for a few and spoke about some show opportunities and maybe some production. We decided to hang out and go clubbing that night. As I said before I don't like to be around a lot of humans, so I didn't go. From what I heard the next day; it was an eventful night. Stabbings and the whole shit. Dudes were wilding out. Krumb was digging the Seven.

He put a show together in Lawrence, Ma. Seven Headed Angel was set to perform. We had a fly routine all set to go. We were ready to show Krumb's squad how we rocked. There were a few performances before us. But as fate would have it, right as they were announcing us a crew of wild Cambodians started a beef and began stabbing people. The next thing that happened completely blew my mind.

Krumb Snatcha looked at his man and said, "Form a circle around God V and protect him". Then Krumb and his Man jumped into the beef. I was bugging on the fact that I didn't even know this dude but on the strength of my music he told his squad to form a circle around me. Yo!! that shit was crazy. They really surrounded me. I said, "Yo I'm good. I don't need protection". I walked out of the circle and stepped onto the stage. I grabbed the mic and started yelling at the Cambodians for fucking up my night. That was a crazy event. I don't know what happened to Krumb's music situation after that. We never linked up.

Chapter Twenty-Three
The S.H.A Album

We took all the profit from the E.P. and purchased better equipment. The Radio Shack microphone taped to a broomstick and placed inside a Poland Springs watercooler jug to keep it upright wasn't going to cut it anymore. What do you know about pantyhose stretched over a wire clothes hanger for a pop filter? We picked up a bunch of gear—a new microphone and mic stand, another Fostex DMT 8 multi-track recorder, a vocal compressor, and some effects modules. I still use that same microphone today. With our upgraded setup, it was finally time to start working on the full album.

Ricky made sure he was involved with this one. He appeared on the first two songs we recorded. *Stahr Wars* featured Ricky and Ralz, while *Earth Angyl* included Ralz, Ricky, and me. Greg Shell, who was close to Saadiq, reached out to see if we wanted to record at Harvard University. He offered to arrange it, and we figured it'd be cool to test out the Harvard studio with Earth Angyl, which was still in its blueprint phase. When we arrived with my EPS, we struggled

Sky King

to connect our hardware—their setup was just as primitive as ours. Greg, who didn't have recording experience, had assumed the Harvard studio would be ready to roll. He saw brothers making positive moves and just wanted to help. Greg's a good dude; I've known him since first grade. He taught me how to tie my shoelaces back in 1981.

At that point, I wasn't even planning to be on "Earth Angyl," but when we got back to my mother's house to record, I decided to jump on and wrote a verse.

Earth Angyl

You're like my starlight, sunshine
ignite the power
sun shower, rain light
bring forth the sunflower
it was mine you held
when we refined ourselves
I refined you
keep in mind I was refined too
Allah knew I would find you
and complete it all
he said we'll both escape
before the meteor falls
and splits the Earth in half
we'll smoke weed and laugh

The Great Solar Stance

don't crash, I'll keep you up at night
and teach you math
so we can rotate
and if I'm ever not there
I'll just regenerate
and watch the God reappear
because you know cash and cars
are outshined by the stars
I'll give you everything
and build a palace on Mars
relax finally, we could unite
and build a dynasty
Honestly
I let your physical astonish me
your mind is overshining me
overshining me
exotic scents of a variety
Things will bloom
coming through the Goddess's womb
your day is soon
luxurious nights up on the moon
like when we all gather
four months away from June
diamond-ring anniversary trips
to Neptune
and you can have it all
I mean this whole entire ball

Sky King

that we're living on
fuck little bullshit at the mall
scientific, quality time
is explicit make me burst
when U n I verse

    Saadiq, Ralz, and I were working on music at the spot when Ricky pulled up in a cab. He told the cab driver to wait and came through like a steamroller. I had this wild beat playing on the EPS, and he immediately said, "I'm getting on that right there... Let's go!" I set up the session, and he said, "I don't have anything written, just some ideas. I'm going in off the top on this one—hit record." I pressed record, and Ricky blacked out on the beat for a few minutes, did some overdubs, gave us all dap, then hopped back in the cab and left. Saadiq added some filler on one part, and that was Ricky's solo joint, *Clock is Ticking*. His momentum was unstoppable that night. If he'd had more time, he would've laid down even more tracks.

    Saadiq's solo, *Sword of Sick*, was another standout on the album. It always got a great response when we performed it due to its energy and tempo. Saadiq is the master of pain rap—struggle rap, hard-times rap, reality rap—call it what you want. He had experienced and seen a lot as a youth, and it all comes alive in his rhymes. Bu's solo joint, Ugly World, further solidified his place as my favorite emcee. Pure, cold-blooded poetry with a solid hook reminiscent of some old-school "Woodsy the Owl" vibe. Crazy.

The Great Solar Stance

My solo track was called *Manchus* (pronounced "Man-Chews," as in biters). Of course, we had to use the scene from "Beat Street" where Pex calls Kuriaki a biter for the scratches on the hook. Mud completely manhandled the cuts on that track. Mud contributed heavily to the album, especially with turntablism, and on *Class of '83*, his scratches blended seamlessly with the beat. That track, featuring Ralz and Bu Ruk, embodied pure B-Boy essence. My personal favorite might be *Lyve & Dyrect* featuring Saadiq and Bu. I knew it was a hit the moment I made the beat. Saadiq and Bu flowed together like interlocking gears—more like brothers than cousins. Saadiq flipped a Just-Ice excerpt for the hook, adding a KRS "La La Luh La La".

The album has sixteen songs, intentionally chosen for numerological reasons: once again 1+6=7, and **Seven Headed Angel** has 16 letters—symbolizing knowledge and equality. We wrapped up with a bonus joint featuring emcee Chilly G, the unofficial official mayor of New Bedford, straight out of Westlawn projects. Chilly has never written a rhyme, freestyling off the dome since 1980. Known as Mark Bark, Chilly Smalls, Chilly Goatmilk, Chilly Gunsmoke, and Boogie Down Bark, he's best known for The Bounce—his signature dance no one else can replicate. Chilly's spontaneous rhymes are unmatched and one of my biggest inspirations. He is a Wild Kingdom legend.

Ultimately, we chose not to title the album. It became known simply as the S.H.A album, or THE Album. I'm not

Sky King

even sure if we consciously decided against giving it a title—we just didn't.

Chapter Twenty-Four
The 3rd Eye Open

Other crews were gaining popularity just like we were. Busted Fro and Lethal Package were putting out music, while Betrayl and Black Shinobi formed a crew called Ikendyenow. If I remember correctly, Betrayl told me the name came about after they recorded a fly joint. When listening back, one of them said, "I can die now," and it stuck. Our four squads quickly became the most prominent in the area. We dropped our album, and everyone knew we weren't playing games. People started asking me for beats left and right, but they specifically wanted Seven Headed Angel beats. I refused to give my best music to rappers outside our crew because I was always working on new projects. We consistently kept fresh music on deck, and Ralz was always eager to record something new.

Ricky would have moved in with me and my family if I'd asked him—these guys were dedicated. We were performing regularly, trying to get our name out there. Around that time, Ben Gilbarg and 3rd Eye were organizing a huge event at Buttonwood Park called the 3rd Eye Open, a celebration of

Sky King

Hip-Hop culture showcasing graffiti, breakdancing, DJing, and emceeing. They even provided free pizza for attendees. Ben asked us to headline the performances, and we eagerly accepted. We prepared a serious routine and couldn't wait to perform.

On the day of the event, which I think ran from noon to 8 p.m., I arrived around 1 p.m., and the place was already packed. Graffiti artists were creating impressive pieces, and basketball games were also underway. From the moment I arrived, people kept asking me when we'd perform. I'd simply reply, "I don't know." I knew we were doing something right when numerous people told me they came specifically to see us, requesting certain songs.

The first 3rd Eye Open was amazing. I believe the performance order was Busted Fro, followed by Lethal Package, and then us. Everyone delivered solid performances. I distinctly remember the Spanish girls going wild for Lethal Package. While I can't recall every detail of our set, I vividly remember Saadiq performing "Sword of Sick," which went down like a cold glass of water—refreshing. He knew how to command the stage. The crowd gave us all their energy, and it felt like the entire city was there. We put our stamp on it that night. 3rd Eye provided New Bedford with a positive celebration of the art form, and that was a beautiful thing.

Chapter Twenty-Five
Amherst

A bunch of us went to a show at UMass Amherst. We were rolling several cars deep. I rode up with Spank, my brother Boo, and Jason—who by this time had already transformed into Jah Born. When we arrived, we all met up in one of the parking garages. As we walked through, we stumbled onto a little rhyme cypher. Someone was playing music from their car, so I threw in a beat tape I'd brought with me.

The guys rhyming said they were from Connecticut, and we dove right in. Our man Dez from Staten Island was with us, and Dez could get busy with the rhymes. He didn't have a Wu-Tang vibe; he had his own unique style. The Connecticut dudes were loving my beats. Dez dropped a killer verse, then I went last. One of the guys from Connecticut was staring at me, looking completely dumbfounded.

When the rhymes wrapped up and the weed was finished, we were getting ready to head up to the event. That's when the dude who had been staring pulled me aside and said I was one of the illest emcees he'd ever heard. That stuck with me, I never forgot it.

Jah Born had brought his video camera, and everybody took turns filming. Not too long ago, he sent me footage from that trip, and part of the cypher was caught on video. You can even see the Connecticut dude talking to me just as we were leaving.

After leaving the parking garage, we headed toward the event. As I walked down a long corridor, I distinctly heard Pop the Brown Hornet's voice. GP Wu was performing that day, and I swore I heard him shout, "Peace to Seven Headed Angel." What?! A few guys walking with me heard it too. When we entered the venue, we saw Dez by the stage talking to members of GP Wu. Everything immediately clicked—these guys were Dez's people. They shouted us out about five times throughout their performance.

We ended up hanging out with Raheem from the Furious Five. At one point, someone slapped a N.O.R.E sticker on the back of Rareform's jacket, and everybody was calling him NORE all day, he had no idea why. That shit was nuts.

Chapter Twenty-Six
Two Giants and the Birth of Sky King

Ralz and I decided to create an album together. This one would get a title. We called it *Two Giants Crushing Mad Mountains: The Wonderous Thunderland Album*. Ralz had transformed into Rah King shortly after we finished the S.H.A album. It didn't take us long to complete the project; Rah was always eager to make music, and I constantly had new beats ready. Ricky was incarcerated for most of the recording process.

During the project's creation, 3rd Eye announced the Secret City Showdown Rap Battle. Rah King and I immediately signed up. The rhymes were to be off the head. Written material was not permitted. I wanted to know if it was going to be judged or determined by the crowd. If the crowd decided, then location would be a big factor. No matter what I was in it, I just wanted all the facts.

I was told there were going to be judges and when I found out who they were I was kind of skeptical. One of the judges and I share a niece. My brother has a child with her sister. One time I did a show, and I was paying homage to a classic DJ

Sky King

Jazzy Jeff & The Fresh Prince song, "Live at Union Square". The song is a recording of a live performance in 1988. Fresh Prince tells the crowd "If you got AIDS be quiet!!!" and the crowd screams. So, at my show I said the same thing to the crowd. I got the same response. My niece's aunt was in attendance and didn't find that amusing. She worked with Treatment on Demand and was bringing attention to the AIDS/HIV epidemic in the city. I do admit, looking back on it now, that wasn't cool. Back then I was just super arrogant and reckless when I spoke on stage. She reported me to my niece and she in turn told my mother. I have a few family members that died from the disease, so my mom was not happy. She went off on me for a few minutes. I straight denied it.

Knowing she was now a judge; I was convinced I had a disadvantage. I visited Ricky and discussed the battle; he agreed that my arrogance and cockiness might prevent me from winning.

The night of the battle arrived. There were a lot of rappers there. More than I thought would show up. Even dudes from Cape Cod were in the building. My first round of the battle was against Betrayl. When Ben announced our names, the crowd gasped. We were two of the most prominent emcees in the neighborhood. I advanced to the next round. I don't know what happened to Rah King's first round but there was some kind of fiasco that resulted in him being disqualified.

The Great Solar Stance

My next round I battled my man, Walter Grant. I advanced to the next round. My third round was against Ice from Busted Fro. No bullshit, I was sort of shook. I pay attention to lyrics. Every time a crew in the city dropped music, I made sure to get a copy and peep all the poetry. I wasn't concerned with the beats. I just wanted to know what time it was with all the other emcees. I'm a fan of fly rhymes. Ice is a beast, and I felt that Busted Fro wasn't allowing him to go full beast mode. I don't know why but I had that type of feeling. I also heard him get busy off the top before. Ice went first. The crazy thing was he didn't assault me at all. He just rhymed. The two rounds I had before that I went directly at my opponents, so he knew what time it was. He threw me for a loop. I advanced to the next round.

I believe the next rounds contained three emcees instead of two, so I had to go at multiple people. A rapper named Able, and I made it to the final round. We had to go for five or six rounds because the judges were gridlocked. By the last round I had run out of gas. I lost interest in it. Able was the winner. I was pissed that I didn't win but he did deserve the "W". I can't front. But if New Bedford had an Olympic Rhyme Team, I would have been selected to be on it. For the first four or five battles of the night I was cooking.

Rah and I wanted to include a freestyle track on our album. I titled it "*The 9th Visit of the Spontaneous Rhyme*," as it was the ninth song we recorded. At the beginning of the track, I said, "Do you think Rah King is gonna waste his time writing

Sky King

this jewel for you?" Without thinking, my next line unintentionally shaped my future: "Do you think Sky King is gonna waste his time writing this for you?" Immediately after recording my verse, Rah asked, "Who is Sky King?" I responded confidently, "That's me. I'm not God V anymore. I'm Sky King." The name resonated with me deeply; fascinated by the cosmos and universe, I felt **Sky King** perfectly represented my identity. If not for us doing that song, I might never have transformed into Sky King.

Adopting the name Sky King brought new energy. It transformed my outlook on music, beat-making, attitude, religious beliefs, and lifestyle—including my diet and reading habits. Once the Thunderland album dropped, the transition from God V to Sky King was swift. It didn't take long for the name to catch on. Only Joey Crack and Felix still call me God V, while Sharik, Chilly Smalls and Foo Foo refer to me as V God.

When Ricky returned home, it was essential to feature him on the album. We were going through beats and Ricky and Rah both wanted a beat that I wasn't too fond of at the time. I would usually change beats after recording the vocals, so I was cool with whatever beat they wanted. This song was called *Bad Weather*. The verses were dope, and the hook was very strong. The song had a lot of energy. Something about the beat didn't sit right with me. I tried to insert a bunch of other beats, but they only sounded worse. I couldn't finalize the song until I found the right beat. Ricky and Rah weren't having any of it

The Great Solar Stance

and fought me on it. I backed down and we went with the original beat. They were correct. That beat was the right choice. I would always get rave reviews about that song when it dropped. Now, I couldn't see that song with any other beat.

Rah had an idea for a song about New Bedford. He already had the hook. I chose to write my verse about Westlawn. This song was recorded before my Sky King transformation. I wanted to rewrite all the verses I recorded as God V, but I didn't have the time. In some cases, I inserted Sky King wherever I said God V. This is a God V rhyme from *En Bee*.

En Bee

It was 1975
when God arrived
I was born in Wild Kingdom
where mad niggas strive
white people were barefoot
niggas played ball
Ricky Gonzalez
threw up burners on the wall
 I used to hang with his brother Paul
he taught us all
to play football,
jump ramps and never fall

Sky King

I heard Nathan's mother call
I used to hang out in the dark
when Chilly Smalls' name was Mark Bark
check Mudfoot on the other half
it makes me laugh
but it was there
where he learned to spin the phonograph
look at Shaft with a hole in his cheek
ask his nephew Sharik
how much liquor
can this nigga drink
a lot of cribs used to stink like piss
that's how it is
Unirockdome on the wall
just ask Biz
the night that Blowfly died
I almost cried
looking out the window
Joan stabbed him in his side
I heard they brought him back
on the helicopter ride
he tried
and fought for his life to be revived
Gary Costa's joints were fat
you know that
back when Karen Mendes
used to go with Warren Rat

The Great Solar Stance

look at Uncle Beef
sucking the bottle straight through his teeth
fast relief,
get drunk to soothe the grief
got all my people strung out on dope
they can't avoid
check the foreigners
all getting punched by Ivan Lloyd
99 percent of the mothers
were unemployed
self-employed Boys Club
niggas B-Boyed

I had created this gritty-sounding beat when Rah came up with another hook idea—he was truly on his A- game for this album. Rah wanted to remake *Why Have I Lost You* by Cameo, and it felt only right to have Ryan Tavares, son of Chubby Tavares, sing the hook for us. Ryan was officially part of the original United Front.

When Rah first introduced the concept, I was hesitant. Sometimes Rah's explanations confuse the hell out of me. But when he arrived at the studio with Ryan and they demonstrated the hook, I immediately saw his vision.

I'll admit, I'm not the easiest person to collaborate with—Ricky and Rah will back me up on this. If I think an idea is weak, I tend to dismiss it outright and won't give it my full attention. That doesn't mean everything I make is great; I've

Sky King

created plenty of lame tracks, but I just leave those on the cutting room floor. I'm always striving to innovate, even though sometimes reality falls short of my vision.

In the end, I fully supported Ryan's version of the Cameo hook. In fact, I believe my verse on that track was the first rhyme I wrote after declaring myself "Sky King."

Lonely Kings

Check the most amazing
words I've ever spoken
announce it to the kingdom
Sky King has awoken
your planet will be broken
broke along the creases
outline the continents
get smashed into seven pieces
bang out your speakers
why are you tracing my angles
your base is star spangled
my foundation is triangles
point at the stars
and put them in jars
we're the fireflies that light up the mics

The Great Solar Stance

at Madi Gras
because you love the
original Bacardi King
move your body girl
check the way I'm partying
look at my mic swing
I'll bend your mic stand
stop all that nonsense
Or I'll chop off your right hand
you'll get your Nikes ran
you couldn't see the lightning
you heard the whole album
went home and started rewriting
you couldn't be frightening
you wouldn't have me scared
it would only get exciting
as soon as God V's nostrils flared
the fire breathing dragon
dried up the rain cloud
Indian rain dance
they scream the name loud
it's just a tribal affair
Saadiq was there
he's King Az Iz
blast these kids no one was spared
he used to be the Icing
I'm Viktorious the Viking

Sky King

mic-ing up every word
computed for your liking
just let the fruit ripen
as I remember nights
of shooting niggas up
with seven billion megabytes

May the Universe be pleased with Ryan Tavares. Rest in peace. We ended the album with a last-minute addition. I wanted to add something hard. I came up with a joint called W.C.W (Wack Crew Warning). The WCW was a wrestling league in competition with the WWF before it became WWE. The plan was to implement a wrestling theme. I like ferocious hardbody B-Boy music. Rah was with it.

W.C.W (Wack Crew Warning)

Sorry suckers just blab a lot
and swear they have a lot
of fresh rhymes
but can't fuck with the seventh astronaut
the God from Camelot
split the Round Table
invincible armor
rip up the sound cable
who goes against
the Great Sky King

The Great Solar Stance

makes the melodies
on a violin string
everything is conducted
under maximum force
it's the ageless backbreaker
thunderous track maker
pile drive your rhymes
off the turn buckle
smash your mountains, your mic
and crush your knuckles
where are your hustles?
you rhyme about pistols
where are your diamonds son?
them shits are really crystals
I'm the headless horseman
on the mic with seven swordsmen
shatter you
your rhymes are made of porcelain
it held the ashes
of your dead mic
I burnt your fortress
Sky King left it scorching

Verse Two

Sky Kingdom in the projects
burn your townhouses

Sky King

smash them
with a stiff seven roundhouses
shred your trousers
crouching tigers
crumble your stone
and crush mountain hikers
anywhere the mic is
and all biters
you can't fuck with
the seven song writers
blast the iron palm
and choke your talents
challenge it
I keep it balanced
I'm the great Atlas
the great Tony Atlas
body slam your rhymes
like wild wrestling matches
bones are cracking
check out the main attraction
Sky King grappled
with the great Bob Backlund

    My cousin Aaron approaches me out on Chancery Street. He tells me he rhymes and that he's in a crew with Bu Ruk's little brother Ebony. They were called Mental Aspects. I told him to come through with Ebony so we could work on

The Great Solar Stance

something. After Aaron had recorded a verse guess who shows up at my spot? None other than Tapski. Tap is Aaron's cousin also and they were tight.

Tap comes up and asks what we were doing. I already knew how this was going to go down. Aaron was eager to show Tap his verse. I hit play and was waiting for the bomb to drop. Tap started laughing and said, "Get off Prodigy's dick". Aaron looked like he wanted to fight. Tap came in and crushed his entire vibe. I knew the feeling. He had done it to me. It only made me better. It would make Aaron better also. Aaron didn't return to make any music for about 2 years. But when he came back, he came back better.

Chapter Twenty-Seven
Solo Albums

Rah King wanted to make his solo album. He was a man of the people, always linking up with the most random cast of characters. You never knew where in the city he might show up, he was everywhere. It was his moment, and he was on fire creatively. He stayed writing, and I was always making beats, so we started another project. The album was titled *The Ending of Forever - Back Down to Earth, Freedom of Speech*. Rah wanted a double CD, twelve songs on each disk, and I agreed.

Rah was hanging out a lot with Travis during this period and asked me how I felt about Trav featuring on a few tracks. I told him we'd try a song first and see how it went. Travis used to rhyme with my cousin Mic Slick in a group called Straight Up Butta. Back in 1994, I put out flyers on Chancery Street challenging any emcee to battle—Trav and Mic Slick were the only ones who showed up. Travis featured on a song called *Tell A Cop*. And I had to admit; he killed it. The song turned out great, and he ended up featuring on two or three more. This

The Great Solar Stance

became Rah King's pattern: whoever he was hanging with during album creation would appear on the album or become part of a new crew. Rah is the illest.

We kept cranking out tracks. I sampled a Curtis Mayfield song for a beat, wrote a hook and a verse. After recording, I noticed my voice sounded deeper and hoarse, though it sounded normal in conversation. I figured I might be getting sick and brushed it off. Rah wrote a verse for the track, and Ricky said I should always rhyme with that voice, though I explained it wasn't intentional. The song was *Entahtainment*. The same vocal change happened again on another track, *Slej-Hammer*. After performing both songs at the 2002 3rd Eye Open, my throat was killing me, but I ignored it.

Bu Ruk came through to feature on Rah's album. I put on a beat that was perfect for him, and his verse was so strong I knew instantly it would be the highlight of the album. Bu mentioned he had another verse ready, so I put both of his verses on the track, sandwiching Rah's verse in between—I always need symmetry in my song structures. Mud started messing with a KRS-One acapella and scratched "The Gods Must Be Crazy" from *Hip Hop vs. Rap*. We named the track *Take It How You Want*. It exemplifies the essence of Seven Headed Angel music—the intense vibe I strive for whenever I create serious B-Boy tracks.

Showtime called me about an Ensoniq ASR-X beat machine, asking if I knew anything about it. Familiar only with the ASR-10, I hadn't heard of the ASR-X. Showtime offered it

Sky King

for free, having acquired it brand-new from someone at the bar. They wanted some of that Late Night White. It was Ensoniq's version of the Akai MPC. I connected it to my EPS via MIDI, doubling my sample time and giving me 32 instrument tracks. Its factory sounds were solid, but I mainly used it as a drum programmer. Inspired by this new setup, I started my own album, *SkyKingdom: Fireball Music*.

The first song that I recorded would end up as the intro to the album. *The Greatest Love* is another off the head joint. I finished it with a sample of Shazan saying, "The Greatest Love". He was seven years old. This is when I started writing verses for Zan so he could learn to recite with rhythm and confidence.

I was really starting to love producing more than emceeing. I wanted to put more focus on production for this project. I asked Dez, Ricky Four, Ice, Bu Ruk, Saadiq, Vizion and Rah King to be part of it.

Jah Born was the DJ at WSMU 91.1 now. He did the introduction to "Unbreakable" featuring Rah King. This track is a sure shot on the album. We were going to perform at a showcase in Worcester, Ma. So, we chose to do *Unbreakable*. Now, I don't let anybody from the squad leave the crib with unreleased music. I hate when joints are leaked because it lessens the impact on the release. When the crew before us was getting ready to rock the DJ accidentally put on the instrumental for Unbreakable for about ten seconds. The crowd went crazy. I heard dudes saying "Oh Shit... What is

The Great Solar Stance

that?". I wanted them to say that when we were on the stage performing it. We still had a solid showing, but the response would've been stronger if that impact was there. Unbreakable is dope.

Ricky Four came through with *Truck*. Whenever I record with Ricky, I'm always trying to get him to channel the Ricky Culture from Truck. That song is the epitome of what Ricky C stands for. Bu Ruk splashed on *Priceless* and *Pearl Harbor*. Pearl Harbor is probably the hardest joint on the album. After the CD came out people would always bring up Pearl Harbor when talking to me about the album.

Saadiq and I did *Monster Mash*. We both used the term "monster mash" in our verses without planning it. I had to call it that. It was only right. Monster Mash is hard. Now that I'm thinking about it, that joint is no joke. Mud contributed a lot to that song. I miss us all being in the same room working on music. We were young and we had all the time in the world. That album wrapped up 2002.

We went to 91.1 to make an appearance on Jah Born's show. Saadiq made it very clear to me that he didn't want me to speak recklessly on air. He said my arrogance could turn people off so we should just let the music do the speaking for us. He was right and I agreed. I toned down the wild rhetoric. A few of us were drinking and swear words were slipping out left and right. The powers that be called Jah Born and told him to stop the vulgarity or the show would be shut down. Jah gets off the phone and explains to us that the interview can proceed

Sky King

but we can't curse anymore. We agreed to be more vigilant with our word choices. Moses, who was shattered, says on the mic " I just got one thing to say". He paused for a moment and then he blurts out "FUUUCK!!". Jah shut down the show and that was the last time we ever went to 91.1

Chapter Twenty-Eight
The Korg Triton

Sweets approached me about producing an album—not for him to rhyme on, but for the dudes in his circle who supported the Seven. I was on board. Rah King was ready to spearhead this project; he was always in go mode.

My cousin Aaron, who rhymes under the name Anti (pronounced "an-tie"), was sitting with me in his red Ford Taurus when he mentioned he had a hook he wanted to sing. I had no idea he could flex his vocals like that. He'd improved his rhyming skills since the last time I heard him. I wanted to feature him on the Sweets mixtape. He recorded two solo tracks: *Training to Die* and *How Much*, which turned out to be among the flyest joints on the mixtape.

Aaron and I were in the studio going through beats when he mentioned he wanted to call his man Dave to ask him to buy me a Korg Triton. Dave believed in Aaron's talent and was already investing time and money to help him realize his dreams. I told Aaron not to call Dave because that sounded crazy. But Aaron called him anyway. "Yo Dave, instead of buying beats for me, you should just buy Sky King a Triton, and he could make more beats than you'd get for the same $2,500." Dave told Aaron to have me call him the next day, and he'd take me to wherever Tritons were sold. What?! I couldn't believe it. Dave was going to buy me a Triton? I performed at a few shows Dave promoted, and we had a good rapport, but I'd never have imagined asking for a favor like that.

Dave showed up the next day and took me to Rick's Music in Swansea. The whole ride, I felt uneasy. Dave didn't owe me anything, and I hadn't even wanted Aaron to make that call. Inside the store, I told the salesman we were looking for a Korg Triton Studio Edition. He brought one out, and Dave asked if I needed anything else. Anything else? The salesman chimed in, "Are you sure you don't want to grab an Akai MPC to go with the Triton?" Dave looked at me, waiting for an answer. I wasn't comfortable with Dave buying me the Triton, let alone an MPC. I told him the Korg was enough. Dave assured me that if I needed the MPC later, I could just let him know. I was blown away by Dave's generosity and couldn't fathom why the universe kept connecting me with people who supported my creative expression.

I knew Ice used a Triton, so I asked him to give me a tutorial. He came by my crib and patiently answered all my questions. I had the manual to fill in any gaps. With the Sweets mixtape wrapped up, I wanted to start working on a new Sky King album using beats I'd make on the Triton.

The Great Solar Stance

Mud, Spank, and I were at my spot chilling when Mud decided to head home. Five minutes later, Mud called my crib saying Paul Coombs must have been in a car accident near the NAACP building because an ambulance was on the scene. Spank and I rushed over there. When we arrived, Ebony was down on one knee as the ambulance was just pulling away. It wasn't an accident—Paul had been shot while sitting in his car. Spank and Paul were close, almost like brothers, tight since childhood. Paul had just come home after serving a ten-year bid, which made things tense since he had been convicted of shooting Barry's brother Zack. Barry and Paul had many mutual friends, making Paul's homecoming complicated. Everyone at the scene rushed to the emergency room for updates. Suddenly, Paul's mother screamed, "Who killed my son?" The atmosphere instantly turned tense. People began whispering that Barry might have been involved. I saw Spank's demeanor change, anger filling his eyes. Soon, people started mentioning Kyle as the shooter. I try to stay out of other people's business, so I had no idea they had issues—I thought they were cool. Hearing Kyle's name shocked me. I was good with Kyle, Paul, and Barry.

Later, while we were putting finishing touches on Sweets' mixtape, someone suggested Spank do the outro. Spank agreed and spoke his mind openly. It created some friction because Kyle had contributed to the Seven, but Spank was a grown man, and I couldn't tell him how to feel. This wasn't a Seven album. This was Sweets' joint. Sweets himself had no issue with the outro.

John Barros, Big A's younger brother, told me he had someone he wanted me to meet—a guy from his school who made music. I trusted John and knew he wouldn't bring any foolishness around, so I told him to come through with his man. He introduced me to Ronnie Johnson, who said John had put him onto Seven Headed Angel. Ron felt we shared a similar mindset about music. We talked setups and exchanged ideas, though it wasn't until sometime later that Ron, and I linked up again.

Chapter Twenty-Nine
The Day The Earth Stood Still

I was getting busy on the Triton. It was time to start working on music. I traded in my Fostex DMT-8 and bought a new Tascam 2488 Digital Porta Studio recorder. This gave me eight more tracks and a whole host of different effects. I gave one of the Fostex joints to Mud. I was going to name this new Sky King album "The Day the Earth Stood Still". The first song that I recorded was called *Holes in the Wall*. I was going to keep the tradition going and go off the head for this joint. I got Bu Ruk to get on it. When I told him it was going to be an off the dome joint, he wasn't with it. He said he had two verses loaded and ready to blast off. I said fuck it and still went off the head.

Holes in the Wall

KRS said duck down
and it broke niggas' backs
I battled seven niggas
and did a backspin on the wax
the furious movement had them all tuned in

Sky King

ready to lose
the magnitude of the words
blew the heels from off his shoes
brace for impact,
the battery pack is so brutal
I spit the fiery birth of Hip Hop
from off the noodle
cut him down
he smacked face first onto the ground
they searched for remains of his verse
but none were found
look at my graffiti,
paint the theme music It's for the needy
no equal, he came with his people
he can't defeat me
eat a mic stand
or snack on a spray paint can
his man ain't saying no words
I'll break his hand
I'll use my boss' van
to roll over you niggas like Berber carpet
rhyming about sweet shit
fucking up the market
with that pasteurized rhyme
that was raised on grain and grass
I said nigga I'm tired of
smashing your mother's ass

The Great Solar Stance

Bu Ruk laid down both of his verses, and I sampled some Eddie Murphy lines from *Trading Places*. This joint was fly—one of my favorite tracks I've ever made. But this album also includes one of my worst songs ever, called *Starscream*. I genuinely hate this track and can't imagine what made me think it belonged on the album. It's a poor representation of my artistry, and I hope I never hear it again.

This album does contain songs that I am proud of. *Touch the Sky* is also one of my all-time favorites. Chops Turner is the son-in-law of one of my mother's best friends. Chops is a soul/r&b singer that performs professionally all over the country. I asked him to get on a song and he obliged. He came to my apartment and asked me what I expected from him and what I was looking for. I told him that my plan was for him to come off the top over the loop of the beat. I really expected him to just give me melody runs. What I got was a whole lot more.

I told him the title of the song was Touch the Sky, and he said his nickname was Adlib. I hit record and Chops went headfirst for a good four minutes straight singing about touching the sky. His display was so dope that I kept the entire take.

Anti and I recorded our verses, and I placed them in just the right spots. The arrangement of the song is so perfect I couldn't believe that Chops chose the correct number of bars between his phrases and his runs that our verses fit perfectly. His phrases became the hooks, and his runs were the melody

Sky King

under the verses. I did not alter his one-take off the head recording at all. The way it is on the song is the way he recorded it. I removed the loop and arranged the beat to accommodate the structure of all the vocals. The way all the components fell into place is unbelievable. *Touch the Sky* is a classic in the catalogue of my creations.

Shazan is nine years old, and he has a solid grasp on reciting rhymes on beat. It was time to put him on wax. I named his song *Shazan Shallah* after his actual name. This song set him on a path to the world of emceeing. He would perform anywhere without hesitation. Ben Gilbarg asked him to rock at a few events. The dopest thing in the world was watching my nine-year-old son rocking a stage. The last song I recorded for this album was *Dreamscape*, inspired by a vivid dream during the making of this album. I tried to capture that imagery as clearly as possible:

Dreamscape

Sky King entered the room
and everything was made of glass
right down to the walls
and the furniture was brass
no carpet on the floor
just tree roots and grass
a flash came through the room

The Great Solar Stance

like crazy stupid fast
it materialized into a man
he held out his hand
and handed me a rhyme book
then said I wouldn't understand
the handwriting looked like mine
but with an ill design
it was a form of graffiti
that came from a different time
he said it was one continuous rhyme
he explained it was the greatest rhyme
that I would ever write
throughout my prime
as I opened up the pages
to this beautiful thing
the composition was entitled
The Musical King
then I flipped through the pages
and recited the words
it multiplied in strength
and broke the world in thirds
when I stepped on continents
and made them surrender it
right there I woke up
and I couldn't even remember it

Sky King

Spank, Ebony, and I were at the park in the Front when Shaft rolled up. He had recently gotten out of Ash Street Jail. He said he had a notebook filled with his "ballistics". Shaft asked when I'd get him in the studio—I told him immediately. Shaft, in his late fifties by then, is a legend of Wild Kingdom, known for his unmatched energy, style, and slang—the true mayor of Westlawn projects. The four of us went back to my place, and just before recording, Shaft requested inspiration: he said, "Put on a porno!" We laughed, but he was serious. I popped in a smut VHS, and Shaft laid down a wild freestyle, blending singing and rapping about street hustling and pimping. I titled the track *Brian Mendes*. New Bedford's west end wasn't ready for it.

Although there are joints on this album I genuinely love, overall, it doesn't resonate deeply with me. It feels like someone else's work, not fully capturing the essence of Sky King. It sounded rushed. I was still searching for that perfect creative pocket to express who and what Sky King truly represents.

While I was mixing and finishing the album, Anti and I were going over some of the music. Shazan runs in the house and says that there is a guy outside pointing a gun at a woman. Anti and I rush downstairs to find all my kid's friends at my front door. I tell them all to get in my house. Anti comes downstairs with my samurai sword. I said, "What are you going to do with that?". I look across the park and see a dude leaning back in an ill stance pointing a shotgun at a woman's back. She

The Great Solar Stance

is on her knees crying with her hands on her head. He isn't saying anything to her. They are just there in broad daylight. I called 911.

I was hoping that this dude did not blast her at point blank range. That shit would've been nuts. The police arrived in no time. Guess who the first officer on the scene was. Officer Nathan Monteiro. My partner in rhyme. MC Nate. He was with officer Dave Conceicao. The same Dave Conceicao that was doing the James Brown dance at the Future Stars 88' talent show. When the cops arrived, the guy dragged the woman into the house. They entered the apartment and apprehended the dude. He was a wild Cape Verdean. I don't think I ever saw him around before that. Anti and I went back upstairs to work on music, and the kids went back outside to play. That shit was crazy.

Chapter Thirty
I Came to Destroy Your Civilization

LeRynn and Saejzan were seven years apart and sharing a room, so we asked United Front to place us in a four-bedroom, and they agreed. In 2005, we moved to 117 Court Street. Anti helped me carry all my furniture. It didn't make sense to rent a moving truck since my new apartment was just two units away, a short three-minute walk. The new apartment came with a playroom, which I repurposed for my music. Although it didn't have a door, the space served its purpose.

I sold my Tascam recorder, the 16-track Tascam mixer, and the Ensoniq ASR-X and invested in a computer with Pro Tools. Recording each instrument track into Pro Tools in real time and manipulating the WAV samples elevated my music production significantly. My song arrangements became more intricate, and I felt like my new capabilities were boundless—though in hindsight, I realize that was merely because I didn't know any better at the time.

One day, Rah came through with Mantis, whom everyone called Fat Marcus. Rah was trying to persuade me to start a new

The Great Solar Stance

Rah King project when Mantis said, "Yo, Sky King, niggas are saying you fell off."

I replied, "What? Nigga, I will kick you out of my crib right now for talking crazy like that." We laughed, wrapped up the conversation, and then they left. But the comment stuck with me, motivating me to immediately start working on a new Sky King album titled *I Came to Destroy Your Civilization*. The title dictates the direction of the sound. Once again, I had to keep the tradition going. The first song would be an off the dome joint and I called this one "Cuz Fat Marcus Said Niggas Think I Fell Off". That is the actual name of the intro.

Cuz Fat Marcus Said Niggas Think I Fell off

Check the glorious music
hail to the siren
I was born in Wild Kingdom when
Blowfly was wildin' and
that's when Shaft was
banging like graff was
you make me laugh cuz
you don't even know what the half was
you know the beautiful shit
that I've seen with my eyes
I've seen baby Hip Hop
spread its wings and rise

Sky King

I don't understand how you
believe niggas' lies
niggas rhyme about murder
and you're surprised when he dies
going to jail is easy
I'll just commit a crime
try staying on the street nigga
and not doing time
niggas be bragging
because they're busting shit
and doing bids,
but yesterday they was on punishment
ask their mother, my name is Sky King nigga
there is no other
there is no God in the sky
cuz God is in my mother
in my sister
and my motherfucking brother
God is in my father,
fucking with the God is like jumping in lava
nigga ask Bu Ruk
that nigga wrote Pearl Harbor
mega producer
call me super creole
but I don't eat no munchupa
the cops... (This is where I messed up but bounced right back.)
Ahh Shit nigga... straight off the dome

The Great Solar Stance

They say Sky King you can't rhyme off the dome
They say Sky King you're always home
They say Sky King you don't know the streets
They say Sky King you fell off on the beats
They say Sky King you fell off on the mic
They say Sky King you got them old ass Nikes
and they say Sky King...Sky King... They're always saying Sky Kiiiing!

I decided to keep the take even though I messed up at one point because it captured the authentic energy of the moment. Fat Marcus had unknowingly ignited a fire in me.

I knew Anti would feature heavily on this album, as he was always around when I created music—he'd earned his seat at the table. For the cover art, I found an image of a spacecraft above a ruined cityscape—perfect for the theme.

One of my favorite tracks from the album is *A Glass Flame*, featuring Saadiq. I sampled Jack Black's vocals, and the result matched exactly what I'd envisioned. I wish Saadiq had the drive to make more music. I'm not sure if he knows how fly his lyrics are.

The album featured everyone from the Seven, though I only performed on eight of the twenty-one tracks. Working with Pro Tools allowed me to be more creative on the production side. I had a bunch of emcees at my disposal, so it was easy to fall back on rhyming.

Sky King

I experimented a little with this one. Ricky Four and I got a song called *Horsepower*. This is different from everything we have done before. We needed to be aggressive and push the envelope.

I wanted to tell a story with one of my verses on this album and Ricky Four opened the window for me. He laid down a verse on a random beat, so I came up with a hook and wrote a verse for *One to Grow On*.

One To Grow On

The world is ugly
got young niggas saying "nobody loves me
nobody put their arms around me
and tried to hug me"
he could be a microphonist
if he would only survive
he's been living on the streets homeless
since he was five
he don't look to the sky
it is such an apparent lie
he don't believe in a God
that let both of his parents die
he was struggling
but not no more this nigga is juggling

The Great Solar Stance

two ounces of coke and some trees
this nigga is bubbling
selling coke to feens
that bring it home to their babies
bullet stricken toothless monsters
were pretty ladies
once, he's starting to lace it up in his blunts
he gets drunk, sucking in the pipe
blowing out his fronts
the demonic deadly tonic
leaned him to the needle
got to support his habit
he's eager to kill some people
just like the older lady
that he caught in the dome
seen her at the ATM
and then he followed her home
his ratchet's out now
her husband's hatchet's out now
chopped off his gun hand
and smashed him in the mouth now
where's all the dreams
that he aspired to be
he's waking up facing murder
in the highest degree
society don't even want him
they gave up on him

Sky King

put him under the jail
and put a grave up on him
the ones with just numbers
no names up on 'em
the devil hovers above
with flames up on him

Bu Ruk and I collaborated on *Jewelry Box*. Anti, Rah King, Ricky, and Shazan each had solo songs. Even though Shazan's name isn't Vernon, I still called him Junior, Sun, or Sunshine. When I found a sample by the Persuaders singing "You make the sun shine in my life," I knew instantly I'd flip it for Shazan. This would be the last song that I would write for him. He started writing his own poems when he was around ten or so.

This album was going according to plan. I was saving all the Pro Tools sessions to a folder on my desktop. Every day I would tell myself to get a thumb drive to store all the sessions. My internal hard drive was almost at capacity, and I was being lazy. That was a recipe for disaster.

I had done a rough mix of all the songs and burnt them on a CD. While watching The Five Heartbeats, I heard a piano that I wanted to sample. I whipped up a beat and laced it with a Bu Ruk verse that I had in the stash. This song became *Footwork*, the last song on the album. I did a rough mix and put it on the CD.

As fate would have it, the very next day my computer froze on me. Without even thinking about the folder with my

The Great Solar Stance

sessions in it, I did a system restore. When the computer restarted, the folder wasn't there anymore I almost shit a brick. It felt like the sky was falling. It felt like the walls were caving in on me. I put in a ridiculous amount of work creating that album. Twenty-one songs down the drain. Then I remembered the rough mix CD. I played that shit a million times trying to convince myself that the mix would suffice. It was going to have to be the final product. I had no choice.

Rah put me on to his man from Providence that printed CDs and covers. When I linked up with him to pick up the album, I noticed that he mispelled Civilization as ***Civilzation*** on the actual CD. I pointed it out and he had to eat that. He gave me the two hundred and fifty CDs for free. I only had to pay for the covers. I was cool with it. I wasn't selling them. I was giving them away to whoever wanted them. First off, I make music for myself. The process is my therapy. Second, I make music for the culture. If my generation doesn't show the next ones how it's done, then who will? I have never sold a Sky King album. They are my gifts to the universe.

Chapter Thirty-One
Rkeyology

My man Frankie was bringing Rah to Ron's spot, and they asked me to go with them. Ron's set-up was light years beyond what I was working with. He was totally digital. At this point I'm using Pro Tools, but my production was still analog. I was recording the Triton into Pro Tools in real time. My instruments were limited. Ron was using Cubase and VST instruments. His sampling capabilities were infinite compared to the Triton.

It might've been the day after my trip to his house when I called him and asked what I needed to get a production station like his. Without any hesitation he told me that he would set up my CPU with Cubase and I would have access to all the magic. WHAT??!!?? I kind of just met him and he is going to put me on like that? Word. This dude is a blessing. His generosity changed my life.

This is the technology that will make my vision a reality. Pro Tools 6.8 required the M Box interface, but Cubase wasn't

The Great Solar Stance

compatible with the M Box, so Ron gave me his old interface. He loaded up my computer with more than I hoped for.

Software, drum breaks and all types of fly shit. I wished that I had the lost Pro Tools sessions to the ICTDYC album so I could go back in and apply this new technology to the music. It broke my heart that I couldn't.

Chapter Thirty-Two
Civil War

In the three years that I lived in the Court Street apartment before creating the I Came to Destroy Your Civilization album, I worked on all kinds of projects, mostly with Rah King. He was always ready and had plenty of material, which probably looked like favoritism, but it was simply due to his abundance of ideas. After the Civilization album, Rah and I collaborated on Just for the Money. As I'm writing this, I'm listening to Just for the Money for the first time since 2009, and this joint still hits hard. I'd forgotten how good it was. Rah and I put significant effort into it, and I'm proud of that project.

After that project, Rah approached me with an idea for another album featuring himself and T Whyte, a local artist known for his singing and songwriting. Since I enjoy incorporating melodies into my tracks, I was immediately on board. This project was different from our previous collaborations. Typically, Rah would record his vocals and leave me to arrange everything alone, which I preferred. However, when finished, he'd sell CDs on the streets without giving me my share of the profits—a fact I often teased him about. When we did "Just for the Money," I split manufacturing costs with him but only recovered my initial investment. I wasn't going to fall for that again. This time, Rah and T Whyte teamed up and paid me upfront before the album's release, which made more sense to me. Even though I previously mentioned I never sold a Sky King album, that didn't mean I shouldn't be compensated for my work on someone else's project.

I was eager to work on this new album, having accumulated beats I wanted to use. Everything unfolded exactly as we'd planned. We recorded daily until all vocals were done. There's no better feeling than seeing all the musical pieces come together. Listening now, there might be a track or two I don't love, but overall, the album was solid. They decided to call it *Definition of the Streets*, featuring appearances by Betrayl, Anti, and Ricky Four. After completing this album, Ricky approached me about producing a "Ricky Culture" album. He offered to pay, but under one condition: I had to follow his direction. Since it was his project and he was paying, I agreed. This marked the beginning of the Ricky Four versus Sky King war.

Ricky and I immediately dove into his project, which proved to be a mistake. While I always had numerous beats ready, I preferred using fresh ones specific to each project. We started only a day or two after finishing Definition of the Streets, making beat selection challenging. Ricky wanted the same energy from the Definition album, but I had already used all the standout beats.

I whipped up a beat that sounded like it was from the 1950's on some doo wop type shit. This would be the first song we did. It was called *Brand New Bag*. This shit came out crazy. I thought we were off to a good start. The next few joints we did weren't as powerful as Brand New Bag. We started butting heads like we usually do but this time I couldn't just delete anything that I didn't like. Ricky gets hot when I go against his ideas. He wants this to be a Ricky Culture album, not a Sky King album. I fully understand where he is coming from. He is paying for a Ricky Culture album. The problem is he wants the Ricky Culture album to sound like a Sky King produced album that's not made the same way Sky King produces an album.

We were always at odds. Rah King peeped what was going on and jumped in and tried to quarterback a few songs. These joints were dope, but Ricky saw the play. Us three were walking to the bodega on Cottage Street after recording some fly shit and Ricky let Rah Know that he wasn't going to run the show on his album. I could see Ricky getting discouraged because his vision isn't coming to fruition.

For the fifteen or so albums that I built before working on Ricky's, I had total control. If there is a hook or anything that I don't like I would not use it. I don't like to invest time and effort in things that don't inspire me to dream about the outcome. I didn't have that power on this one. It was just a

The Great Solar Stance

matter of creative differences between Ricky and me. Don't get it twisted. There are fly joints on that album. The collective of songs was not his vision. We never put that project on the street.

I'm with Rah at the baseball field next to Presidential projects and he tells me that Ricky Four is not a fan of mine. Ricky told him that I ruined his career. I immediately called Ricky's crib and when he answered the phone I said "Yo.. this is the nigga that ruined your career". He said, "Fuck You" and hung up on me. We didn't speak again for about a year.

During that time Rah asked me to produce his Black Dynamite album. He wanted to build an album based loosely on the Black Dynamite movie. I figured I would make the beats from samples of Adrian Younge's *Black Dynamite* soundtrack. At this time, I had moved out of United Front and bought a home in the south end. Ricky and I end up connecting again through Rah King.

The first time Ricky came to my new crib we showed him some of the Black Dynamite joints. That blew his top and he was pissed at me again. He felt he got slighted because how could Rah have fly shit before the Ricky Four album? His shit comes out mediocre, then Rah has fly shit after his album. Ricky is thinking there is no explanation for this other than Sky King sabotaged my shit. Even though Ricky and I have never had any kind of beef that would explain the reason for a sabotage job. Ricky even told me that I intentionally fucked up his album because I knew it would be better than my albums.

Sky King

That didn't make any sense. Rah King's first album is better than my first three solo albums. If I got to make a Bu Ruk joint, it would have been better than all my projects.

I kept telling him that it was the process. All I need is an emcee to come to the crib, record all the vocals and then just leave. That's it. I don't want to hear any ideas or any directions at all. You might say "Sky King, how do you plan on making songs for people and not accept any of their input?". It's easy, I just make songs without considering anybody's input. On all of Rah King's albums that I have done, he just records his vocals and then leaves. When he comes back, the song is done and that's it. There might have been a handful of times that he didn't like the final version of a song. I would try to convey this to Ricky but based on the optics of the situation, it looked like favoritism.

I never felt a sort of way about him being mad at me. I just wish he would've trusted me to quarterback his album. We went another length of time just arguing every time we spoke. I didn't let Rah release the Black Dynamite album. I wasn't impressed. I found it to be silly. Some joints were dope, but the vibe seemed gimmicky. Two albums in a row I felt were sub-par. Something got to give. I came up with a plan. I would merge the future and the past.

Chapter Thirty-Three
Seven Headed ARSTO

The ARSTO crew was the new generation of west end rappers that came up behind the Seven Headed Angel. Chiz Mac and Siahlaw were the prominent emcees of the squad. I really didn't know the depth of their roster. Chiz is family and Siah was formerly known as Black Shinobi from the Ikendyenow crew. Later, I found out that my brother Kippy's god son Teff Banga was affiliated with them also. My idea was to make an album merging Seven Headed Angel and the ARSTO Entertainment Music Group. I wanted to strategically place members of both groups on songs together.

I had done some music with Chiz and Siah so I asked them if they were willing to participate on this joint album. They agreed so I began formulating a blueprint. I knew the Seven squad would be down for it. My brothers are always ready if I reach out.

Siah introduced me to Low Da Ox and Bino. These two dudes showed up every time I asked them to get on a joint. It was hard work trying to get Chiz on songs. I got the feeling

Sky King

that she didn't like to over saturate anything with her presence. She wants her persona to be sought after. If you give the people too much, they won't look for it anymore. I could dig it. I finally got her on a joint with Anti called *Luv Letter*.

I rhyme on three songs. My family and I were starting to notice that my voice was getting a little froggy. The distortion was enhanced when I rhymed. This started in 2001 and gradually got worse over the years. I limited how many songs I would appear on. I didn't have any discomfort, but I started to sound like a cigarette smoker, and I never smoked cigarettes.

There was one song that I had to get on. Siah showed me a beat his man Iron Mike had made, and he told me about a concept he had. (B.L.A.C.K) I **B**elieve that **L**ove **A**lways **C**reates **K**ings. Fifteen minutes after Siah left my crib, I called him and told him that my verse was done.

B.L.A.C.K

It's like a young black girl
meets a young black boy
from the start, give her the world
she'll fill his heart with joy
that love is blacker than the universe
or the first woman's womb
it's blacker than the view
inside a dead king's tomb

The Great Solar Stance

it's deeper than that though
we've fallen in a black hole
remember crowns yo
wrapped around a black afro
back then a man was
blacker than a man now
look what his hand does
it makes a fist, he held it up proud
above his seeds
a man's deeds will help the future bloom
but his absence in it's life
only prepares it for it's doom
fuck that boom and that bap
we built more than rap
we build a nation of kings
then we blow them off the map
that goes against every law
the universe has written
it's older than the pyramids
it's older than religion
remove all the little kids
from ghettos that they live in
and show them all the beauty
that is held in deep within them
BLACK IS BEAUTIFUL

Sky King

Iron Mike gave me the OK to recreate his beat and that song came out crazy. I was playing this album in the background as I'm writing this and I'm realizing how dope this entire project is. This was a solid rebound after making two that I thought weren't my best expressions.

I called this album *An Unstoppable Force Meets an Immovable Object*. This is my lane. Constructing songs the way that I see them in my head is my favorite thing to do. I only require vocal stems. If I had a group of emcees that had the capability to record their own verses and send me the files, I would be banging out songs on a regular basis. Music creation is my release. I've tried to stop making music. That shit lasted about two weeks. I tried to start focusing more on reading, which is my second love, but I just couldn't stay away from it. Whether I would be making songs or not I would still make beats daily.

Occasionally Anti would come through and we would talk about making his album. We were going to come from a different angle with his joint. It was going to be an R&B vibe. I couldn't get him to slow down enough so we could get started. He was constantly making moves. If you know Anti you know he kept it pushing. He ended up staying with his pops in Yarmouth. I barely got to see him once he moved out there. I ran into him down south end and he made me feel like I was slowing him down. He knew that I knew what time it was, and he just wasn't trying to deal with me dropping jewels on him.

The Great Solar Stance

The next thing I hear is how he got down on some wild shit and tried to rob 7Eleven and got arrested. Rah King just happened to be going to court the same day as Anti's arraignment and was in the bullpen with him. Rah got released and came and found me. He told me that Anti sent a message for me to hold down his daughter.

My son was doing a little stint behind the wall and called me to tell me that he saw Anti on the inside, but he didn't seem like himself. A few days after that I was at work when I got a call from Sha King. He said he had heard that Anti had killed himself. I was chalking that up to people in New Bedford running with wild stories. Sha seemed convinced. I told him that I would call Aaron's mother then call him back.

Anti's mom answered the phone, and I asked if Aaron was ok. Her exact words were "Vernon, no he's not. Aaron killed himself today". That shit hit me like a ton of bricks. I spoke to her for a moment then I called Sha King back. I did not want to tell Sharnae. Her and Aaron were close. This dude was always at my crib. He bought two Pitbull puppies and gave me one. He helped me move twice. If I needed him for anything he would come through. I couldn't believe it. I'm not even sure if he heard the final version of the last songs he recorded.

Chapter Thirty-Four
Golden Soul

It's 2015 and I need a new project to work on. I wasn't in the mood to attempt a Sky King album. The issue that I was having with my voice was killing my enthusiasm for emceeing. I had a concept for an album floating around in my head. I was going to ghost write an album but have other emcees record the verses. I would reference the tracks so they could memorize the rhymes. After pondering that idea for a while I figured it would be too much work.

I was watching OnDemand on Comcast one day and a random video of Grem slaying a rhyme off the head just happened to come on. I had known Grem for at least fifteen years. I had lumped him in with the 3rd Eye community and never really paid him much attention. His performances were energetic, but I still didn't take notice to his music. That was mostly due to my extreme arrogance. But this video that I watched was different. He made me pay attention. I didn't know he could get busy like that. Ice was his partner in rhyme and together they formed DirtyDurdie.

The Great Solar Stance

Ice was putting out snapshots of music which he called Throw Ups. A reference to quick graffiti tags. They were making noise, had a solid following and a strong stage show. I had been a fan of Ice for a long time. I researched their Dirtydurdie catalogue, and I was impressed. A plan started to formulate.

I reached out and asked if they were interested in doing an album together. They came by my crib and said they were most definitely with it, but they had a stipulation. I had to rhyme on the album, and I had to perform with them. Anybody that knows me knows that I don't make many appearances. I don't care to be around large groups of humans. I explained the problem with my voice, but I agreed to their demands, nonetheless. They left with three beats. When they returned, we recorded *Boom Bap Madness*.

Right from jump I knew this was going to be a banger. If this was any indication of what the album was going to sound like, I didn't think their fans were ready. We were only a few songs in when they booked a show in Providence, R.I. I just so happened to be on one of the first joints we did. This song would be titled *Glass Hurricane* by the time the album was finished. They planned on rocking an early version of the song in their set.

Before it was our time to rock, a rapper from Newport, R.I named Kee Words took the stage. This shit was crazy. The crowd knew all his hooks. The level of crowd participation was unlike anything from around the New Bedford area. He got his shit off that night, and it was effortless. I was impressed. Now it's time for us to get down.

Just prior to starting the DirtyDurdie project I had made a song called *Evil Jesus*. The name Evil Jesus was the new persona I was taking on for a solo album before I shot down the idea. The joint got a great reception from online listeners. It was my atheistic take on Christianity. Evil Jesus is a fly joint. Ice and Grem wanted me to open the set with it. I body rocked the crowd with it that night. The rest of the set went down so crazy that we performed Glass Hurricane twice. Back-to-back.

After we got off the stage, I introduced myself to Kee Words. He told me he was blown away by Evil Jesus. I responded by inviting him to appear on the DirtyDurdie album. They all knew each other. Two white girls approached me and said they hadn't heard anything like Evil Jesus before. They wanted to know where they could find the song. The crowd that night showed me a lot of love. The backpacker underground Hip Hop scene in Rhode Island is dope. I wasn't sold on the beat for Glass Hurricane. I knew I was going to change it. When I found the right beat, we all knew it was the correct choice.

The Great Solar Stance

Glass Hurricane

Intergalactic monuments
monumental instruments
that intimately coalesce
I'm infamously infinite
and intricately assembled
as the sun god of a pagan
that gave birth to a nation
of mentally dead cavemen
I stand on Halley's comet
and build a fortress on it
my eyes scan the horizon
and all things beyond it
demonic forms of energy
multiplied by ten of me
with bionic gauntlets
that crush you telekinetically
Sky King the Viking
Gaiking with the wrist rockets
Grandizer 88'
dislocate your hip sockets
robotic artform
return to seek vengeance
revenge of the deadly venoms
poison your descendants

Sky King

elements and diagrams
blueprint of the matrix
I rocked the golden era
wearing a pair of purple Asics
the greatest on the planet earth
legendary pantomime
Universal Star Angel
transcends the sands of time
I rhyme like the Herculoids
stone age magician
wizard in the pyramid
creator of religion
undiscovered dinosaur
creature on the ocean floor
art official water walking
Jesus that you're hoping for
sky diving space needle
break the tectonics
shape shifting organism
made with electronics
cybernetic sky-net
with the bloodline of a mutant
to terminate your database
with a worldwide pollutant

    Ice had made a solo joint called *Manifest Density*. The main sample had a faint piano in the background, so I asked Ron to play along with it to brighten the keys. Ron went ham and gave me more elements than I expected. I took the stems home and rebuilt the song. The new arrangement was perfection.

I treated Ron's additional instrumentation as samples and manipulated the audio. Since Ron gave me an abundance of ingredients, I was able to find the pieces that I wanted and bent them to my will. This is how I wanted to produce. Arranging audio was the best way for me to exercise my imagination. The same way that I could build an entire universe with words was the same imaginative method I use to create the soundtrack of that universe.

If you can't tell by now, my rhymes are very esoteric. You have to think about what I am saying in my lyrics. I write for me. I don't worry about if you can understand it or not. It's not for you to understand. I understand it perfectly. I use the same approach when crafting music.

I have to understand the feeling of the soundscape. When a beat creates a picture in my mind, that image must coincide with the image that the lyrics generate. Having more ingredients allows for a higher probability of me achieving that goal. I tried to get Ron's input on as many songs as I could. Sometimes less is more. In some cases, I didn't need any extra sauce on the joint. After Manifest Density we did *Try-Angles*. I knew Ron was going to touch this one. This song was on some Anunnaki type shit, so the guys asked me to get on this song also. This sort of new age thinking was right up my alley.

Sky King

Try-Angles

I'm the architect of the matrix
worshipping the stars
in stone villages
I build pyramids on Mars
and leave scars on the planet
I'll carve my face
on the surface with laser beams
shot from outer space
the atmosphere boils
rock turns to oils
24 minerals
extracted from the soils
great space Gods
in escape pods
invasion of your home world
we shot radiant rods
that electrify the water
we engineered the slaves
gave orders to man
and raised them from their graves
take daughters from man
and impregnate their womb
built a stargate
on the dark side of the moon

The Great Solar Stance

and hide the secrets of the cosmos
inside genetic fluids
mapped your genome
and gave the knowledge to the Druids
you silly mortals
don't even see my fingerprints
I wrote it in a rhyme
and put it over instruments
I AM GOD

When I recorded that verse, I had to do it a few times. Not because I was fucking up, but because my voice kept cracking and sounding crazy. The finished version of the verse is me holding in my stomach and forcing out the words with as much strength as I could possibly muster. In 2015 my vocal cords were getting bad. I still dismissed it.

Every song that we came up with for this album was a keeper. Nothing was staying on the cutting room floor. We began to talk about the title of the album. I suggested The Secret Teachings of the Artform. Ice came back with The Golden Soul Comrade. He explained that this album was going to be a B-Boy's(or B-Girl's) companion, his or her comrade. All B-Boys and B-Girls must have a golden soul. You can't be a B-Boy without an understanding of the golden art era of Hip Hop.

We start working on the title track *G.S.C* and Grem recorded his verse first. When Ice laid down his verse it changed the vibe of the song. Grem's verse was solid, but Ice's verse utilized the letters G, S and C. All the words began with a G, an S or a C. In some cases, threeword phrases began with all three letters. God Spark Champion, Great Space Coaster and Genius Sole Controller was how Ice was rocking. I stopped the session and suggested that Grem rewrite his verse to do the same thing so the song will have symmetry. Grem left and came back with exactly what he was asked to come back with.

Ron cut up Danny Ray saying, "Super Dynamite Soul". Danny Ray is the man that introduces James Brown on stage and drapes him with his cape. This is the first song on the album and this shit kicks in the door. Golden Soul Comrade is a pure representation of the artform. I had a looped beat of some classic B-Boy type shit. Grem and I were going to do a joint about Breakdancing. I started to write my verse then I had an idea. I decided to sample *It's Just Begun* by The Jimmy Castor Bunch. Anybody that was an official Break Dancer back in the day had to rock to It's Just Begun at least once.

I cooked up some Beat Street type shit for the breaks and it changed the entire feel of the song. When the guys came over to record, I dropped the new beat on them and blew their wigs back. Ice decided to get on the track. He couldn't let that one get away. The song was titled *Battle Cry*. Of all the albums that I have done, GSC is the most Hip Hop centric. Every album I have constructed was built on the foundation of the culture, but this album is about Hip Hop. It's not just demonstrating

The Great Solar Stance

Hip Hop. It is ABOUT Hip Hop. I had a lot of fun building this project.

My favorite song on the album is a Grem solo joint titled *Credit Score*. There is something about the way the piano sample hits. Grem showed and proved. The rhymes, the hook and the overall picture being painted was on point.

My favorite verse from this album is an Ice rhyme from a song called *G-Force*. Something about this verse resonates with me. So much so, that I had to put it in this book.

G-Force

Hey, Witness how I got 'em mystified
By the guided missiles I exemplify
Gassing up your air supply
when I amplify
Like the sky is my land
and my land is the sky
And I'm walking when I glide
With a dignified stride of an osprey
I can see it all,
its most of yall that lost me
Dipping down the Audubon
Quicker than the trigger
of a firearm
Screaming out Alaikum Salam

Sky King

With the rifle on
safety And I'll be in the lead
When the checkered flag is waving
Probably,
racing for my whole generation
The representation
Of poetry in motion
I don't know stagnation
Shove came to push
I went against the gravitation
Cuz I'd rather go alone
Than drag a broke battle station
Lately it's been sounding Like
it's time for my entrance
They need an overhaul
I brought a brand-new engine
Vroom Vroom
You can hear the horses
Coming down your block
Sounding like a hundred Porches
Looking at me funny
Like I'm on a flying saucer
 Treating me as if my speech
was from a foreign author
Heed warnings
My aura is enormous
He's formless

The Great Solar Stance

That's why they can't box him
Outfoxing him
Will never be your best option
When you think he's sleeping
Nah he's just playing possum
Watching, analyzing
And problem solving
Evolving,
His deep thoughts are awesome
Aliens gave him the eye
Of Steve Austin
Now all he's trying to do
Is feed colostrum to Gotham
And fertilize the seeds
Till a new breed blossom
Arch enemies
saying Someone please stop him
Every time he talks
They can feel their stock dropping
Plus, he do it all
Without a single Glock popping

       -Demmene Syronn

DirtyDurdie had an album release party at The Met in Pawtucket, Rhode Island. This was a few days after GSC dropped and I couldn't believe the reception. While we performed the album people were right up on the stage reciting all the lyrics. I was amazed. How do they know all the rhymes? The album just came out. That shit was crazy. I had done many shows in my life but until that point, I had never peeped anyone in the crowd saying my rhymes. It hit different.

Emcees from R.I started reaching out to me looking for beats. One time I got into a heated discussion on Facebook with this bozo dude that was trying to diss DirtyDurdie. A rapper from Boston hit me on Messenger and asked me if I wanted him to shoot the dude. I told him I was a grown ass man. I don't need anyone to intervene. Dude from Boston told me he had mad love for me. I didn't even know him personally. He was down to clap somebody on the strength of my music. That was wild.

Chapter Thirty-Five
Evil Jesus

While I was mixing down the GSC album I thought about the term "Boom Bap". I came to the realization that I kind of don't make boom bap music. When I think of boom bap I think of drum heavy MPC patterns with a stuttered sample. DJ Premier most certainly makes boom bap music. He just might be the champion of boom bap. KRS ONE has his definition of boom bap as "real hard beats and real rap". I agree with that and though I believe I fit that description most times, my music has a different feel to it.

My inner mind's eye envisions my music as graffiti on a wall or in a black book. I see my sound as an ambiguous motion on display. Colorful paint splashed on a wall. Now I'm sure that any follower of my music can tell if a beat is mine or not. I'm sure I have a specific sound that is embedded in all things I create, but each creation is from a different position within the spectrum. Most times I come from outside the spectrum. I am Hip Hop, I am Rap, I am Graffiti Music. That is the only way that I can articulate my style.

Sky King

After I found the words to define my sound I wanted to express it. I would build off the Evil Jesus persona and make an EP. I get bored with things very quickly, so I didn't want to get involved with an entire album. Seven songs should be enough. The first one was already done. Evil Jesus.

Evil Jesus

Golden cross, golden chain
a crucifix controls your brain I
 wrote it all in the Book of Time
way before the explosion came
I'm Big Bang, you're little boom
with a dunce cap in a little room
I fly across every galaxy
in the driver's seat
on a witch's broom
I built the moon in the Earth's belly
sweet revenge of Machiavelli
my Solar Stance is so advanced
I'm the Malachi Brothers and Fonzarelli
Christians and Catholics
crusade the globe in battleships
I told yall that I don't exist

The Great Solar Stance

but you still believe in those magic tricks
magic sticks, magic wands
I trampled yall on a Mastodon
you built a tower to touch the God
I crushed your power in Babylon
confused the tongues of Nimrod
I'm the Son of Man in the Synagogue
I'm the sun God of the summertime
I'm the sun rise of the winter God
born again on the twenty fifth
Revelation is just a myth
I arrive again on the equinox
and I ain't the one to be fucking with
twelve disciples, twelve tribes
I wrote the book with twelve scribes
twelve signs of the zodiac
I return again to watch hell rise
I AM JESUS

Verse Two

I'm the Sun God, the Sun Deity
a roundhouse and a one eighty
a foot sweep and a back breaker
I'll fuck you up and I'm gun crazy
I'm turning water into wine
won't play a song if it isn't mine

Sky King

I'll give you Cancer, I'll give you AIDS
leave you homeless out in the wintertime
read a book but you ain't a reader
what is faith to a fake believer
the images that you're worshipping
is nothing more than the face of Caesar
the offspring of Alexander
I'm offering propaganda
accept it and the war is over
mighty Thor has dropped his hammer
I'm the morning star named Lucifer
I'm Zeus God of Jupiter
my fingers wear the rings of Saturn
I'm the thinker executioner
I murder those that go against it
I'm man-made I've been invented
no evidence of my existence
but I'm always being represented
the keeper of the Holy Grail
I slaughter men to no avail
I'm riding off on a pale horse
with the bloodshot eyes and a golden tail
so, shake hands with the Sun Devil
you can't escape from the running rebel
the esoteric knowledge in me
is heavier than a ton of metal
I AM JESUS

The Great Solar Stance

I didn't release Evil Jesus as an EP. I released each song individually after it was mixed down. Ron contributed a lot to the production of each song. Just like with the GSC album, he would give me tons of material, and I would reconstruct everything around the vocals. Out of the seven songs, two were stand outs in my eyes.

The Unknown is about the fantastical imaginary thoughts that would go through my mind in the last ten seconds of my brain shutting down just before my death. I sampled a local artist named Tiger Rose. I stumbled across a live acoustic performance of her playing on a friend's Facebook page. I contacted her and asked if she would have a problem with me doing my rendition of her song. She gave me her blessing, so I asked Aaron's daughter Jayliana to do the hook for me. I wanted her to sing a piece of Tiger Rose's lyrics but with her own flare on it. I found Tiger Rose's studio recording of the song on Soundcloud. I got a clean sample of the guitar as opposed to the gritty live cell phone recorded version. "Poetry is the language of imagination" - KRS ONE

The Unknown

I draw a spectacular diagram
of all things in existence
and bathe in the starlight
as I calculate the distance

Sky King

I touched ground on Venus
as the sun reached its zenith
I seen it, as I flew across
on the fiery wings of a phoenix
cinematic visionary
now my life is before my eyes
ten years go by every second
right before my mind dies
hypnotized and timeless
what is the weight of a shadow?
now I'm blind and mindless
as I approach my greatest battle
fire flashes of lightning
illuminated a long corridor
at the end was an alien
that stood beside the Lord of War
and three angelic beings
wearing a bright glowing fabric
they smoked weed and spoke
Aramaic and ancient Arabic
the Lord told me he would show me
the depths of the unknown
fascinated by a beam of light
reflecting off his throne
he ripped the heart from the alien
and replaced it with some stones
he extracted seven jewels

The Great Solar Stance

that were embedded inside its bones
the knowledge of the Universe
was etched inside the crystals
that were hidden from the humans
that shoot themselves with pistols
the most violent and tyrant
plague is the Earth's people
at that moment I realized
the Lord was speaking Hebrew
but I understood his language
how could I understand him?
conversate with a phantom?
my mind became a lantern
and shined light upon
the shattered pieces of a mirror
he told me close my eyes
and his words became clearer

Verse Two

In a sudden burst of energy
matter is being created
from a single singularity
he had showed me how he had made it
he played it like a beautiful harmony
as he blew his horn
I watched a star being born

Sky King

I rode on a white unicorn
he said it was infinite growth
the expansion never stops
he tried to tell us from the beginning
he left the patterns on our crops
he dropped the knowledge on Egypt
and the lineage of the Pharaohs
and the bloodline of Anunnaki's
killed with poisoned arrows
he said an angel in a starship
had landed in Sumeria
and gave a gift to his children
and their knowledge became superior
then a being with a hooded cloak
and a long wooden sickle
waived his hands
and the air before my eyes began to ripple
I said "Oh God I must be dreaming
please save me from this Demon"
now I need him
in all those years
I didn't even believe him
then he appeared in a great flash
the sound of breaking glass
he saved me from the Reaper's clutches
moving crazy fast
we're moving at the speed of thought

The Great Solar Stance

we arrived at seven doors
he said only one can opened
then he said the choice is yours
he said that he never existed
he just lives inside the mind
of the ones who think the truth
is just too difficult to find
he said that he's only showed me
things that I've already known
just pre-existing knowledge
that was floating in my dome
then I walked through the seventh door
hoping to be reborn
but my soul was separated
from my physical form
IT WENT TO BLACKNESS

The other standout song from this EP is called *Welcome to the Space Age*. If I had to pick one song that perfectly describes what goes on in my mind, this would be that song. I have always been captivated by the study of the Universe. Most of the books in my personal library are about Astronomy, Astrophysics and Mathematics. I have a bunch of fiction books but even those are Star Wars novels. The immense size and power of the cosmos, combined with all its mysteries, commands most of my dedicated reading time.

Sky King

When I decided to tap into this subject for this song, I knew the beat had to be correct. After I built a strong but simple foundation for the beat, I wrote to that basic loop. I wrote both verses in one sitting. That writing process felt so organic it seemed like the rhyme was just spilling out on to the page. I only write in an actual notebook with pen and paper. I don't use my phone to write things down. I need to feel the motion of the letters. With the beat playing and my eyes closed, my imagination went into overdrive. A lot of the lines might not make sense to the average listener. But to me, every word is the truest description of how Sky King sees himself and how he sees the world.

Welcome to the Space Age is a depiction of the purest form of Sky King. I recorded the vocals and showed Ron the next time he came over. Ron had a vision for it, and he brought that vision to life. He turned my rhymes over a basic beat into an instruction manual for interstellar travel. The song sounds cosmic. I asked Jayliana to get on the joint also. When all the pieces of the puzzle were assembled, a beautiful mural emerged. I sent the joint to Jah Born and he sent back a video. He made a fucking video for the song. The craziest thing is that I wasn't involved with the making of the video at all, but the video flawlessly captures the meaning of the song. I don't even know where he got the footage from. He fucking nailed it.

The Great Solar Stance

Welcome to the Space Age

It's the undeniable dynamics
metaphysics of mic mechanics
I'm Evil Jesus I feed the people
understand I bring light to planets
super powerful solar rays
burning holes through the hourglass
returning rap to olden days
it's the golden age; will the power last?
I'm the black devil in catechism
world ending cataclysm
ultraviolet x-ray vision
I whirlwind and I shatter prisms
I'm light bending, reading rainbows
life force, do you believe in angels?
biochemical presentations
of aliens in multicolored Kangols
 your soul is ripped from your abdomen
traveling through the quantum physics
telescopic space rockets
invasions of the reptilian lizards
broadcasting the soundwaves
I'm Prometheus to the brown slaves
refine the gold, my story is told
in hieroglyphics found in caves
stargates and space collisions

Sky King

asteroids and great divisions
we escape to the space station
and leave the place where we made religions
the Earth cried, worlds collide
I'll torch your soul, and you'll burn inside
heaven or hell, whatever place you dwell
you deserve to die
WELCOME TO THE SPACE AGE

Verse Two

It's the speed of light in hyperspace
when I arrive, I ignite the place
I time travel, I've been to Mars
and built a laboratory inside it's face
your body is placed into two boxes
to symbolize both equinoxes
we terraformed your entire planet
the atmosphere is for the evil monsters
disconnection of your internet
your Jesus hasn't visited yet
we intercepted his fiery chariot
and had a scorpion sting his neck
kiss of death, face of Judah
we calculate with a great computer
as we approach the Age of Aquarius
I'm Sagittarius, the greatest shooter

The Great Solar Stance

intergalactic observation
plot a course through the constellation
we navigate through the darkest space
with an iron face in deep concentration
telekinetic mind power
apocalypse in the final hour
mathematical algorithms
find Fibonacci's design in flowers
cyborgs and humanoids
everything in the world is destroyed
captain's log, star date
as we venture off into the frozen void
the great God Osiris
is infected with the Ebola virus
the antidote is the words I wrote
on papyrus
WELCOME TO THE SPACE AGE

    I added a song I made about Anti to the EP and that brought the total of songs to eight. I'm pleased with Evil Jesus. I expressed everything I wanted to say in just eight joints.

Chapter Thirty-Six
The Reunion

It's 2016 and Lamont Ferg reaches out about a Seven Headed Angel reunion show. I didn't want to do it, but I still had to ask my brothers how they felt about it. Everybody else was gung-ho ready to get down. That conversation led to us building on doing a new Seven Headed Angel album. I was down to do an S.H.A project but I knew it was going to be hectic. Bu Ruk was living across the street from me at this time. I knew I could get him in the studio whenever I needed him. Everybody else was in close radius. We set up a meeting so we could talk about how we would proceed with the album.

Right off rip we decided that we weren't going to have any appearances by outside emcees. This joint was going to be just us. After we announced the upcoming album, I had to shut a few people down after they inquired about getting down with the program. I felt like my hands were hot. I had some fly shit cooking in the oven. We began recording. From the beginning Ricky and I already started clashing. Our relationship dynamic is crazy. We always had creative differences. Back then we

The Great Solar Stance

would go through it. When we were clicking, we were clicking. When we were off balance, we were off balance. Sometimes our frequencies just weren't aligned. But even when were weren't on the same page he would still jump in front of a bullet for me. Our bickering was just a byproduct of the type of brotherhood we had.

Rah and I were the only ones that kept making music consistently throughout the years, so I felt like my opinion on the direction of these new songs should've held a lot of weight. It must be tough working with me. I'll be the first one to say it out loud. But my track record should speak for itself.

We had two or three new songs by the time the show arrived. Saadiq and I spearheaded the routine for the gig. We tried to incorporate Mud as much as possible. He had a lot of cues to remember. Two things can happen at a Seven Headed Angel show: it's either fireworks and orgasms or it's crash and burn. There is no happy medium. LMAO. It was always difficult to get everybody together to practice. This reunion show was no different. We weren't kids anymore. We're grown men with different schedules and priorities.

The show was approaching fast. We might have practiced twice. I didn't have faith in it. Rah and Ricky had to talk me into even doing the show. Here we are, it's showtime. It was a torrential downpour outside. I didn't think anybody would show up. When we took to the stage nobody could find Ricky. This shit was nuts. Right off the starting block, straight out the

Sky King

gate, cues were missed and the whole shit fell apart. It was a terrible display.

We kept working on the album and recorded a few songs. Rah, Bu and I did a joint called *David Lopan*. Named after the villain in the Big Trouble in Little China movie. Rah and I got a joint called *The Angelics*. Bu did *Pearl Harbor pt. 2* and Ricky recorded a solo joint called *The Great Escape*. He got away from a narcotics raid in '95 by tossing around some cops and running through Mud's building. Ricky climbed the balcony and ran through Mud's apartment. Mud, Spank and I were in his bedroom with David Goya, watching David bag up some cocaine, when Mud's girlfriend came into the room and said Ricky just climbed up the balcony and ran through the house. Two minutes later the Narcs were banging on the door. They ran up in Mud's spot looking for Ricky. Mud's mom's bedroom door was locked so they thought Ricky was in there.

While they were wasting time trying to get permission to enter her room, Ricky was on third floor in the trash compactor room. He jumped out the side window and Ace and Fletch gave him a ride to the north end.

My guy got away clean. Ricky describes this event so eloquently in the song that you could visualize the whole shit with your eyes closed. (I'm going to have to backtrack a little bit. I just remembered a crazy Ricky Four story that is most worthy of being in this book.) This takes place around '94-'95ish.

The Great Solar Stance

Ricky and I were at my crib on Sycamore Street. He gets a call about something to do with his product not being official. Somebody told his plug that his shit was bunk. Ricky was getting his shit prepackaged so the plug was bugging out. Ricky tells the dude that he is on his way back to Beetle Court. He tells me the situation and says that these wild Puerto Ricans are probably going to roll on him. I told him to wait for me to get dressed and I'll go with him.

Ricky calls a cab. We pull up to Beetle Court and there are about ten dudes waiting for him. Ricky jumps out of the car and starts blacking out on these dudes. One of the guys was with his girlfriend. She had to be about nine months pregnant. She was ready to drop that load. Ricky tells these guys that he didn't switch any of the work and that he is going to fight all of them at the same time. I'm standing there like "What the fuck is this nigga getting me into?". We are about to get fucked up. Then he screams "And my man right here ain't even gonna help me!!". These guys start laughing and the main dude tells Ricky that he's out of his mind. Ricky looks at the dude with his pregnant girl and says, "I'll kick your bitch right in the stomach and you won't do anything about it because you're a bitch". That shit blew my mind. I thought we were going to get shot.

Ricky squared up and stared at all of them. They backed down and the main cat said it wasn't that serious. We walked to Ricky's crib, rolled a blunt and laughed. Ricky Four is a different breed. They don't build them like that anymore. That shit was wild. Now back to our regular scheduled program.

In all fairness I do have to say that Ricky was trying to get in the studio as much as physically possible. I think the initial argument that Ricky and I had on the first day of recording turned Saadiq off a little bit. I didn't feel any enthusiasm from him. After the first wave of recorded songs the energy seemed to die down. Even I was losing interest. I think that wack ass show destroyed the vibe.

I had a vision for the album. I wanted to title it *Revenge of the Seven Headed Angel*. I wanted it to be nothing but hard body assassination music. The type of shit that makes you do the stank face. The frequency wasn't resonating correctly.

During this album process my wife was on my back about getting my throat checked out. I made an appointment and met with a Dr. Spongberg, an ear, nose and throat specialist. I was diagnosed with Laryngopharyngeal Reflux. There was a non-cancerous nodule on my vocal cords preventing them from closing properly. I needed surgery to remove the nodule. One wrong move and my vocal cords could be permanently damaged. I chose to go with the surgery.

After the operation my voice returned to normal. But what I found was, if I raise my voice or get excited when I speak, the distorted vocal starts to come back. I had to fall back from rhyming. I wasn't even discouraged or crushed in any way. If I weren't a beat maker/producer also, I most likely would have been devastated. I still had music, and I found producing to be more appealing than emceeing.

Time passed, the idea of a new Seven Headed album fizzled out and I was just making beats. Ron had made a fly beat and reached out to see if I was down to do a joint with Ray. Ray is the super intelligent young bull that gets busy. His poetry is that of an emcee from my generation. Ron wants to call the joint Iconoclast. Since I am an iconoclast, it only made sense for me to get on it. After a lot of deliberation, I talked myself into doing it. My voice came out kind of rough but not as bad as I expected.

Iconoclast

How can an immaterial man
create planets?
how can a virgin
duplicate man's organics?
how can the Earth form
before a star has begun?
the elements of the Earth
are forged in the heart of the sun?
why didn't Egypt
ever document the plagues?

Sky King

who defaced the monuments
and lied about their age?
the zodiac diagrams
the lifetime of Horus
Abraham and Moses
were written during Taurus
who knows the differences
between Zeus and Jesus?
who knows the difference
between his face and Caesar's?
science is the sunshine
sometimes the mind freezes
faith is one of mankind's
most deadliest diseases
complete trust and confidence
with no supporting data
the greatest serial killer
is the trait of your creator
a man-made hologram
contains every answer
who prays to a God
that gives a young child cancer?
who speaks in tongues
and understands the translation?
who's been to heaven
and seen a man's transformation?
who cured him of his AIDS

The Great Solar Stance

and threw away his medication?
he still died of AIDS
in these days of revelation
who believes in magic
and the resurrected fossils?
mechanics of the cosmos
is the story of the gospels
iconoclastic
destroyer of your images
thirty-three degrees
of interplanetary visitors
Astro theological
wizard is from Kemet
stargazer
then a savior was invented
on December twenty second
when the sunrise is the least
for three days the sun appears to cease
out of breath,
on the twenty fifth
it rises from death
one of multiple demises of Seth
a star has risen
a fraudulent king of a new religion
I don't know what he is
but I can tell you what he isn't

Chapter Thirty-Seven
The Holocron

Idle time is the devil's playground. I need to scratch the itch. I need a new project. This time it needs to be something different. I'm a Star Wars nerd. Nobody has ever made a Star Wars themed album before. It won't be about Star Wars. I'll just utilize samples from all the Star Wars content. This one is going to be called The Holocron. In the Star Wars universe, a holocron is a device that stores information in holographic form and can only be accessed by those who are skilled in the Force. I'm a Sith Lord at heart so this album is going to be a Sith holocron, which is tetrahedral-shaped. Before I started working on the album, I ordered a Sith holocron from Amazon and kept it on my desk for the duration of the creation process.

I reached out to Ice and Ray to get on the first song. This ended up being the title track, *The Holocron*. These dudes got busy on this joint. Both slid some Star Wars terminology into their verses in such a subtle manner, that it made the song even more cohesive than I anticipated. When the first song out the starting block is dope, the level of enthusiasm goes through the

The Great Solar Stance

roof. All I wanted to do was get out of work every day and get straight into the studio. I wanted to put everything I had into this album. No excuses or regrets. This is going to be the championship winning season. I'll be able to retire with the trophy and devote all my free time to reading.

Ice, Ray, Siahlaw, Ricky Four, Grem, Kaydaluz, Vizion, 40 Swords, Bu Ruk and Rah King were all brought in to make this dream a reality. I knew exactly how I wanted this project to sound, and it wasn't going to go down any other way. I had announced my latest venture on Facebook, and I peeped some subliminal posts. Motherfuckers that I considered family had said some shit that I considered to be slick talk. Maybe they weren't speaking about me, but I took it that way. That shit was like a propulsion system making me go hard in the lab. Especially when my shit is like the central nervous system in the human body and your shit is nothing but a bunch of fucking tinker toys.

Bu Ruk had recorded a verse about some devilish government type shit while we were working on the Seven Headed Angel album. I put that verse on a different beat and recruited Ice and Siah to add on to the song. This song became *The First Galactic Empire*. I was on a roll. Two songs in and both were serious heat rocks.

Rah King had five solo joints. Out of twenty-four songs, he is on ten of them. He came through for me when I needed him to. Rah was a big part of this project. Kaoss sent me a beat that was on my type of time. It sounded like a classic Seven

Sky King

Headed Angel beat. I put Rah on that and asked EmiliOMG to write and sing the hook. Every time that I have asked Emilio to get on a track he goes hammer time on it. He hasn't disappointed yet.

Kaoss sends me the stems and allows me to manipulate his beats to fit my vision for the arrangement. Ron contributed to almost every song. He came over one day to add on to a Siahlaw joint. He got so busy with his add-ons that I removed everything that I had on the beat and just kept his add-ons. That joint was about some atheism type shit, so I called that one *The Phantom Menace*.

It was all interlocking perfectly. Star Wars themes without being about Star Wars. I recycled Ricky Four's unused verses from the SHA album. Rah and Ricky got a song called *Twin Ion Engines*. That is taken from the meaning of the T.I.E Fighter spaceship. Ricky and Rah have been like Starsky and Hutch since Rah got down with us. I gave it a brand-new beat, and it was ready. Almost all of the vocals on this album were recorded to beats that were different than the final version of the song. That has been one of my M.O's since my Ensoniq EPS days.

One of the craziest joints on this album is *The Force*. I asked Siah and Ray to each give me a verse, but I needed one to be about Light and one to be about Darkness. Ray chose dark and Siah went with light. After they recorded their verses, I came up with the idea of giving them each a different beat. I brought the blueprint to Ron's crib and this dude ended up

The Great Solar Stance

playing the Star Wars theme. I brought the stems home and used that to bridge the two beats together. I put Yoda on that shit, and it was a wrap.

I had an unused Anti verse so I asked Siah to give me a verse that would coincide with what Anti had already laid down. Siah did exactly that. I might have changed the beat to this song five or six times. It was only right that I put Jayliana on this song with her dad. This was his last recorded verse. I expected her to sing something but to my surprise she came back with a rhyme. We went with it, and I let her close out the song on some fly B-Girl shit. She also flexed on a Bu Ruk solo joint singing the Casanova hook.

I would love to do a Jayliana/EmiliOMG album. Some fly soul vocals over melodic Graffiti Music. I would have loved to put Shazan on this album, but he was on vacation at City College. If you're from the streets, you know what I'm talking about. Right from the conception of this project I had planned on it being my last album. Not meaning that I wouldn't make music anymore, I meant that I wouldn't make entire albums anymore. It's too time-consuming. I get wrapped up in the production of it and lose focus on everything else.

The Holocron has twenty-four songs that all had to get produced, directed and mixed. That shit is hard to do when you have a family. But I'm a selfish bastard and my wife always paid the price.

I wrote four songs for this album but only three made it. I completely forgot about the fourth song until after I finished

Sky King

and pressed the album. I forgot another song by Halogen Majesty. Months later I was going through all the session files and realized I never mixed down Halogen's song. I wish I had included it. The only solo joint I had on the album was called *Hyperspace*. I sampled a song called Bulimundo by a Cape Verdean band also called Bulimundo. The original track is fast, so I slowed it down a lot. After I wrote it, I didn't record it right away. Ron came over and sprinkled his magic music dust over the bare bones loop that I had. I used the elements that Ron gave me and rearranged the four-bar sequence. Now that the beat was more complete, I tuned up the lyrics.

Hyperspace

Microphone rocking
no rehearsal
beyond all starlight
universal
graphic novel
illustration
birth of a God
in personification
civilization
man's creation
blind devotion
space invasion

The Great Solar Stance

exploration
travel the length of
you challenged Sky King
but didn't know the strength of
freedom of the mind
generates momentum
trapped behind the iron walls
I bent 'em
you duplicate styles
because you can't invent 'em
where did he come from?
heaven sent him
the world is a shamble
believe the fable
slight of the hand
underneath the table
powerful impact
atomic force
trample your fort
on an iron horse
destroy your fortress
defeat your forces
reveal the face
under Caesar's portraits
cataclysmic
the world is ending
Armageddon

Sky King

your will is bending
good or evil
which are you defending?
who's authentic
 and who's pretending?
the Star of David
who's the favorite?
the chosen nation
is aboard the spaceship
corroded flesh
with a golden bracelet
destroy the Earth
and they can't replace it
a face on Mars
and they can't erase it
King is on the mic
and he always slays it
grand ovation
quantum leaping
the time is now
but the sheep are sleeping
activation
secret agent
watch the explosion
beneath the pavement
molten lava
hot contagion

The Great Solar Stance

spread the virus
destroy the pagan
God is amazing
teach the heathen
reach the sky
And release the demon
fire breathing
white inferno
burn the pages
of that rapper's journal
internal damage
but we manage
break the cycle
and take advantage
bandage the planet
heal the wound
eclipse the Earth
and conceal the moon
shadows loom
you learn the tune
Graffiti Music
is returning soon
burn the fume
we're in the matrix
cultivation
begin the basics
we're in the places

Sky King

read inscriptions
Alien races
teach Egyptians

When the album was completed, I listened to it in its entirety. It needed something. All Star Wars movies begin with an opening crawl that explains the film. I needed an opening crawl and there was only one person that could write it. My cousin TJ (40 Swords) has the perfect vocabulary, wit and Star Wars knowledge to get the job done. I reached out and he sent it back to me in no time. Before I finished reading the first sentence, I already knew this was going to be the intro to my album. TJ knocked that shit out of the park. It was exactly what I was looking for.

This was the ideal album for Sky King. This was the ideal album BY Sky King. After listening from beginning to end I felt The Holocron was the most accurate representation of who and what Sky King is. Sky King is Westlawn. Sky King is Melle Mel. Sky King is Run DMC. Sky King Is Kung Fu Theater. Sky King is Beat Street. Sky King is The Great Solar Stance. Sky King is Sade. Sky King is Rakim. Sky King is 1988. Sky King is Triple Stage Darkness. Sky King is Private Stock. Sky King is These Tu Bum Emcees. Sky King is God V. Sky King is Viktory God Allah. Sky King is a Golden Soul Comrade. Sky King is Graffiti Music. Sky King is The Holocron. My transformation is now complete. Sky King is The Seven Headed Angel.

Epilogue

During the completion of The Holocron, Siah had brought up the idea of us doing an album together. My plan was to walk away with the championship ring and not do any more albums. I wanted to invest time in family and reading books. I had to respectfully decline. Sharnae and I were talking about me not doing albums anymore and I told her about Siah's offer. I mentioned that I wasn't going to do it. She said "You have got to do it. That's Siah. That album would be dope." I thought about it for a few days then contacted Siah and told him I was down for the project. He said that he wanted to call the album *Simatic*. A play on the word cymatics, which is the study of how sound and vibration can be made visible. I found a picture online that seemed to represent frequencies in the human body. Siah asked Eden to recreate the image with certain details. The cover art was my inspiration for the soundscape.

    The intro to Simatic is one of my favorite joints. The beat is a guitar accompanied by classic space movie sound effects from the 1950's. Siah rocked one verse that's on some DMT fueled ride through his own consciousness. My type of fly exotic shit.

Sky King

Simatic Intro

I got the
Tree of Life in my mind nigga
conscious of the prana serpent
like up the spine nigga
earth wind and fire water blind nigga
all the elements that
make up a divine nigga
my soul is perfectly aligned
inside my body though
sequential combination
out the Fibonacci code
I got the key to open portals
try to lock me though
liberate the spirit and the body
can't stop me "no"
sitting in the lotus
as I meditate
supplemental herbals
help me elevate
deep in the dimension
that I penetrate
two opposing forces
when protected will defend the gate
penetrate illusion
using all my chakras

The Great Solar Stance

bathing in DMT
sipping ayahuasca
spinning in the rhythm
of the limitless
my five senses band together
like I'm Hiawatha
it's holographic now
as I hallucinate
focus on my dream
in a lucid state
hone in on my craft
as I move the weight
I begin to love things
that I used to hate
like the plant-based diet
helping Si ascend
I try to curve the light
that my mind will bend
Si's the kaleidoscope
that I shine on them
the tears in the universe
I'ma try to mend
life is like the matrix
and I'm Neo king
death ain't on the canvas
on my easel king
I'm Morpheus

Sky King

and agents never back down
got the blueprint
of Solomon in my background
                    -Siahlaw

We were banging out songs daily. I would email him the beats that we chose, and he would typically have the lyrics ready to record the next day. Two days the most. It would take longer for me to arrange a song than it did for him to write it. I had a song that was meant for The Holocron but I forgot all about it when it came time to finish the album. I showed Siah and told him write a verse for it. The song is called *Art of War*. When I wrote that rhyme, I had no idea that it would be the last rhyme I would ever write.

Art of War

Powerful imagination
time space levitation
mind power is infinite
we calculate its estimation
as worth more than diamonds are
tell me when you find Allah
I'm Evil Jesus Christ
reflections of a shining star
burn all your daydreams
halogenic laser beams

The Great Solar Stance

Sky King is the all-seeing eye
he writes amazing themes
navigate the thunderstorm
the day the sun was born
illuminate the human race
and make them hunger for him
iconoclastic atheist
pi times the radius
I'm Seven Headed Angel God
I crucified the satanist
I hard dap the hands of time
magnetic mastermind
I autograph the cosmos
and wrote my name in Nazca lines
sunshine, summertime
encounters of another kind
my mind built a time warp
I multiplied the number nine
soul sonic force field
of liquid vibranium
we are Tasmanian devils
with teeth of titanium

    The song count was getting crazy. I called Siah and asked what he thought about making two albums. At the time of this phone call, we had twenty-something songs completed. We ended up doing forty songs. The second album would be called

Sky King

Overlord. When I think about these two albums, I see Simatic as light and Overlord as dark. A perfect balance. I brought Ron in on most of the songs. Having that extra instrumentation to manipulate during arrangement is so invaluable. If I had to define the vibe of these albums I would have to say, "Scientifically Mystic". It was a great experience doing these two projects and I'm happy that I listened to Sharnae. She is always right.

www.ingramcontent.com/pod-product-compliance
Lightning Source LLC
Chambersburg PA
CBHW072042160426
43197CB00014B/2599